To
Muhlenberg College

Rrrg Jahan
April 5, 2008

THE ELUSIVE AGENDA

Rounaq Jahan is currently at the School of International and Public Affairs, Columbia University, New York. She was previously Professor of Political Science at Dhaka University, Bangladesh (1970–82), and headed the Women's Programmes at the UN Asia Pacific Development Centre in Malaysia (1982–84), and the International Labour Office, Geneva, in Switzerland (1985–89). She received her PhD in Political Science from Harvard University. Her publications include *Pakistan: Failure in National Integration* (Columbia University Press: New York 1972); *Women and Development: Perspectives from South and South East Asia*, co-edited with Hanna Papanek (BILIA: Dhaka 1979); and *Bangladesh Politics: Problems and Issues* (UPL: Dhaka 1980). She has been involved in the women's movement over the last two decades, and participated in the World Women's Conferences in Mexico (1975), Copenhagen (1980) and Nairobi (1985). A founder of Women for Women, a pioneering research and study group in Bangladesh, she is on the advisory board of *Human Rights Watch: Asia, Asian Survey* and *Asian Thought and Society: An International Review*.

THE ELUSIVE AGENDA

Mainstreaming Women in Development

ROUNAQ JAHAN

UNIVERSITY PRESS LIMITED
Dhaka

ZED BOOKS
London & New Jersey

This book is being made available to relevant organizations, libraries and individuals in the South free of charge as a result of the generosity of the Royal Ministry for Foreign Affairs, Norway

The Elusive Agenda: Mainstreaming Women in Development was first published by Zed Books Ltd, 7 Cynthia Street, London N1 9JF, UK, and 165 First Avenue, Atlantic Highlands, New Jersey 07716, USA, in 1995

The Bangladesh edition was published by Mohiuddin Ahmed and produced by The University Press Ltd, Red Crescent Building, 114 Motijheel C/A, PO Box 2611, Dhaka 1000, Bangladesh, in 1995

Cover designed by Andrew Corbett
Typeset in Monotype Garamond by Lucy Morton, London SE12
Printed and bound in the United Kingdom
by Biddles Ltd, Guildford and King's Lynn

A catalogue record for this book is available from the British Library
US CIP data is available from the Library of Congress

ISBN 1 85649 273 7 Hb
ISBN 1 85649 274 5 Pb
Dhaka ISBN 984 05 1272 2

For my sisters: Roushan and Nilufar
and my brothers: Kabir, Karim and Munir

CONTENTS

LIST OF TABLES AND FIGURES

PREFACE

The world has witnessed a remarkable surge in the women's movement over the last two decades, which has put forward a bold vision of social transformation and challenged the global community to respond. This study reviews the response of one set of key players: the international donor agencies dealing with women's development issues. It focuses on the actions of four donors, two bilateral (Norway and Canada) and two multilateral (the World Bank and the United Nations Development Programme), analyses their impact in two specific countries (Tanzania and Bangladesh), and compares donors' priorities with those of their development partners.

This study attempts to synthesize the experiences of the last twenty years in broad strokes. Such an assessment is needed as we prepare for the Fourth World Conference on Women in 1995 in order to address the question: Where do we go from here? I realize that the experience of four donors and two countries gives us only a partial view, based on limited data. Development assistance is a fast-growing field, and it is possible that major shifts will have occurred in a few years. But an assessment of experience, however limited, provides an opportunity to take a step back, analyse common patterns and trends, reflect on the lessons learnt and think about the future. This book is written in that spirit.

In analysing past experiences, I have used the perspective gained from my being both an 'outsider' and an 'insider': I have been outside, involved in the women's movement; I was also inside for a limited period, working in multilateral agencies. This study highlights the aspirations and roles of the women's movement as well as the actions of the donor agencies and governments, attempting to identify both their achievements and their shortfalls.

I outlined the research for this study in 1989, but started collecting data only during 1991–92. The analytical framework and some of the findings of research were presented in a seminar on Mainstreaming Women in Development (WID) organized by the Expert Group of the Development Assistance Committee (DAC) of the Organization for Economic Cooperation and Development (OECD) on WID in Paris in May 1992. The first draft of the manuscript was prepared in the summer of 1993. I later revised it for publication in the spring of 1994. The revision benefited from the insight and information I gained in being involved in the OECD/DAC's evaluation of DAC members' WID policies and organizational measures during 1993–94.

This study is intended for several audiences: donors and their counterparts; women's organizations; nongovernmental organizations (NGOs); and research and training institutions. Though women's organizations and NGOs have struggled to put women on the development agenda, they have limited access to agency and government documents, and this lack of information often generates mistrust between insiders and outsiders. This book, which draws heavily upon the donor agencies' unpublished documents, is written in part to disseminate information about the donors' strategies to a wider public, thus bringing greater transparency to the donors' work.

Many institutions and people have made this study possible. My first debt is to the Norwegian Agency for Development Cooperation (NORAD), who funded the research for this study. NORAD also facilitated my data-collection efforts in the donor agencies and the partner countries. I would particularly like to thank Elisabeth Eie and Randi K. Bendiksen, who first decided to fund the study, and Bjørg Leite and Ingebjørg Støfring, who later urged me to expand it. Ingebjørg Stofring was especially helpful in locating data and documents and remained an enthusiastic supporter of the project throughout. Zakia Hassan and Roar Wik also greatly facilitated the study. My interviews with NORAD officials in Oslo, Dhaka and Dar-es-Saalam – particularly with Per Ø. Grimstad, Sven A. Holmsen, Ingrid Øfstad, Gerd Wahlstrom, Bjørg Merthe Luis, Terje Gran, Tør Larsen, Tove Reite, Froydis Aarbakke, Hilde Johansen, Idar Johansen – helped me gain an insider's perspective on the workings of NORAD. Else Skjønsberg, Janne Lexow, and Anne Grimsrud provided valuable critiques of NORAD. Britte Hilde Kjöläs kindly provided gender-disaggregated data.

The officials of the three other donor agencies were also cooperative. At the Canadian International Development Agency (CIDA) headquarters, I am grateful to Elizabeth McAllister, Marni Givran, Barbara Brown, Catherine Wolfrey, Rebecca Macphail, Françoise Mailhot, Linda Moffit, Sefora Masia and Nadia Kostieuk for sharing information and ideas with me. CIDA resident representatives in Bangladesh and Tanzania were very open with their ideas to me. I would also like to thank Maureen Ahern Blais of Corporate Memory who provided statistical information. Maureen O'Niel of the North–South Institute kindly facilitated my contacts with CIDA officials, for which I remain grateful. At the United Nations Development Programme (UNDP) headquarters, I am grateful to Ingrid Eide, Elizabeth Reid, Elizabeth Lwanga Okwenje, Gustaf Edgren, Sarah Timpson, Renue Chahil Graff, Jocellene Bazile Finley, Lina Banerjee, Nancy Yates, Somendu Banerjee, Johan De Graff, Andrew Villeneuva and Linda Schiber for their help in facilitating my research. UNDP resident representatives in Bangladesh and Tanzania also co-operated with the study. At the World Bank, I would like to thank Barbara Herz, Gotz Schreiber, Lynn Bennett, Monica Fong, Elizabeth Morris Hughes, Rekha Dayal, Loretta Schaffer, Rashida Chowdhury, Katherine Winter and Maritt Wiig for their help in giving me access to data and information. I would like to thank Stephanie Baile, Tara Gildea and Karl Wahren at the OECD in Paris for their assistance with my research. The Bureau of the Expert Group on WID of OECD/DAC was particularly helpful in giving me good feedback on my preliminary ideas.

In both Tanzania and Bangladesh I benefited from discussions with numerous people. I would particularly like to thank Sarwari Rahman, Gule Afroz Mahbub, Salma Khan, Farida Akhtar, Jowshan ara Rahman, Ayesha Khanam, Wahida Huq, Khushi Kabir, Sufia Islam, Md. Yunus, F. H. Abed, Rehman Sobhan, Enam Chowdhury, Shwakat Ali, Mama Kisanga, Fatma Alloo, Marjorie Mbilinyi, Bertha Koda, Naomi Katungi, N.Z. Tenge and Mariam R. Halfen.

Joann Vanek and Mallica Vajrathon helped in locating documents. Ruth Dixon gave valuable comments on my research proposal. Hameeda Hossain, Roushan Jahan, Ahmad Kabir and Anna Gourlay read the draft manuscript and made excellent suggestions for improvement. Nilufar Ahmad helped in the preparation of the tables. I am grateful to them. I also thank Humayan Kabir who typed the manuscript through its various stages.

Various friends in the New York area – Adrienne Germain, Joan Dunlop, Judith Bruce, Florence Howe, Mariam Chamberlain, Talat Jafri, S.A. and Ayesha Karim, A.M.A. and Sabia Muhith, Leonard Gordon, Philip Oldenberg, George and Sondra Zeidenstein, Susan Davis and Sidney Jones – made my stay in the city enjoyable. I am particularly grateful to Susan Davis who first drew NORAD's attention to my research proposal.

Columbia University provided me with an academic home and excellent hideout for writing the book. I am especially grateful to Dean Ainslee Embree for suggesting that I take up affiliation with Columbia for the project. I would also like to thank Dean Robin Lewis and Jack Hawley, Director of Southern Asian Institute for their support all through the project. Barbara Gombach, Bob Cessna and their crew of work study students provided a friendly atmosphere at the Institute, for which I am grateful.

As always my mother and my sisters and brothers have been extremely supportive of my work and my nomadic life style.

While many institutions and individuals have helped in the research for and production of this study, I alone am responsible for its contents and views.

Rounaq Jahan,
New York, May 1994

CHAPTER I

INTRODUCTION

We want a world where inequality based on class, gender, and race is absent from every country, and from the relationships among countries. We want a world where basic needs become basic rights and where poverty and all forms of violence are eliminated. Each person will have the opportunity to develop her or his full potential and creativity, and women's values of nurturance and solidarity will characterize human relationships. In such a world women's reproductive role will be redefined: child care will be shared by men, women, and society as a whole. We want a world where the massive resources now used in the production of the means of destruction will be diverted to areas where they will help to relieve oppression both inside and outside the home.... We want a world where all institutions are open to participatory democratic processes, where women share in determining priorities and decisions.... Only by sharpening the links between equality, development, and peace, can we show that the 'basic rights' of the poor and the transformation of the institutions that subordinate women are inextricably linked. They can be achieved together through the self-empowerment of women.

Gita Sen and Caren Grown, *Development, Crisis and Alternative Visions: Third World Women's Perspectives*, New York 1987, pp. 80–82

It was nearly two decades ago that the global community affirmed gender equality as a central developmental concern, and a decade ago that it adopted Forward Looking Strategies (FLS) to accelerate women's advancement. In the last twenty years, in response to the demands of the women's movement and the United Nations mandates, national governments and international development agencies have adopted special policies and measures to promote women's advancement. 'Women in development' (WID) emerged as a visible field of policy and action in most of the international development agencies and in many countries, especially those which were dependent on foreign assistance. The United Nations organized three world conferences on women – in Mexico in 1975, in Copenhagen in 1980, and in Nairobi in 1985 – and is poised for the fourth in Beijing in 1995. It is time to ask: what have been the achievements so far? How have the various policies and measures adopted by the international agencies and national governments functioned? Have they been effective in promoting women's advancement and gender equality? Have the world's women witnessed significant improvements in their living and working conditions over the last twenty years?

Evidence suggests a mixed record. On the one hand, sustained advocacy has led to greater understanding and awareness of gender issues. Women's organizations and networks have multiplied. The women's movement has gained in strength. Women's agendas have been more clearly articulated – equality, empowerment and the transformation of existing development paradigms have emerged as critical issues. Governments and international agencies have adopted more mandates and policies and implemented a variety of actions. Protest movements and grassroots initiatives have shown alternative paths to development. On the other hand, data also indicate that inequalities have grown between the North and the South; between the rich and the poor. In the last two decades, more women have joined the ranks of the world's poor in both North and South. The cutbacks in social services as a result of structural adjustment policies, and the increased incidence of crime and violence, have hit poor women the hardest. Women's responsibilities as sole or primary income-earners have increased, their labour-force participation rates have grown, but the workplace has not made significant changes to accommodate women's needs, and continues to exploit women as cheap labour. Economic desperation has led to unprecedented female migration and an increased trafficking of women and children worldwide.

The most recent *Global Survey of the Role of Women in Development* summed up the impact of the 1980s on the world's women as follows:

> If the global economic situation in the 1980s is examined in aggregate terms, it has been one of the longest periods of growth ever recorded; but ... development, as it has been understood in its broadest sense in international development strategies, has not been occurring. This is particularly true for women. The evidence shows that while some have improved their position through improved access to employment and more remunerated economic sectors, far more have become poor. Ironically poverty among women has increased even within the richest countries resulting in what has become known as the 'feminization of poverty'.[1]

If the 1980s have not been favourable to the majority of the world's women, what are their prospects for the 1990s? Again, there are contradictory trends. Women are faced with challenges of ever greater hardship, but they are also presented with increased opportunities to bring their perspective to bear in shaping the future development agenda. The emphasis on market-oriented policies, the opening up of markets by the General Agreement on Tariffs and Trade (GATT) and heightened competition between countries for market share are likely to result in an intensification of the current policies and practices of exploiting women's unpaid and low-paid labour and using them as a reserve labour-force. The rekindling of old ethnic rivalries, war and fundamentalism raises the prospects of greater violence against women and more out-side control over their bodies and choices. On the other hand, the growing strength of civil society and the movements for democracy, human rights, people's participation and the environment are likely to create a bigger space for women's voices in determining the direction of development. How can the global community guard against the negative trends and foster the positive? What strategies should be followed in the 1990s?

In charting future directions, we need to review our past experiences and draw lessons from what has worked and what has not. This study is an attempt to assess the experiences of one set of actors – the inter-national donor agencies – who have played a critical role in shaping both the global development agenda and the specific WID policies and measures. It seeks to elucidate how WID policies and measures have worked in different settings – in donor agencies as well as in their partner countries. The study investigates whether these policies and measures have been successful in achieving their aims and in meeting the aspirations of the women's movement. It is not intended to be a detailed evaluation; the experiences of both the donors and their counterparts are analysed to illuminate the key issue explored by the study: why has progress been so elusive for women? What explains the contradictory trends – a heightened advocacy and awareness of gender issues on the one hand, and the growing poverty of the world's women on the other?

To aid our understanding of these achievements and failures, the study examines several questions: How should progress be measured – by WID efforts or results? What explains the gaps between the inten-tions and the impact of WID policies and measures? Is progress elusive because women's agendas have not been clearly defined, or is it because policies and measures have not adequately addressed that agenda? Are WID policies and strategies essentially on the right track, needing only more time and better implementation, or do they need reorientation?

WOMEN'S AGENDA

When the United Nations declared 1976–85 the Decade for Women and Development it created high expectations, particularly among women in the South. It was hoped that the international development agencies and national governments would provide leadership in giving guidance and undertaking proactive measures to address the root causes of gender inequalities. Since civil society was relatively weak in the Southern countries, the fledgling women's groups that were interested in development issues in the 1970s made the state and the international development agencies a prime target of their advocacy efforts. The international agencies and national governments slowly responded. Typically they set up what has come to be known as 'special machineries' for women – women's ministries or bureaux in national governments, and WID advisors or units in international agencies. These machineries devised policies and strategies, and implemented actions. They supported research and special projects, developed guidelines, organized training, introduced special procedures and tools, and funded women's organizations. These multifaceted activities enhanced knowledge and understanding of gender issues, increased gender expertise within agencies and governments, and strengthened the voice of women. But it became increasingly evident that the international agencies and their development partners were bypassing a large part of the women's agenda.

The choice of the three major themes of the Decade for Women – equality, development and peace – already signalled a comprehensive agenda. The Plan of Action debated in Mexico in 1975[2] and the Forward Looking Strategies adopted in Nairobi in 1985[3] included a wide list of issues encompassing the total spectrum of development. While the breadth of issues sometimes made the women's agenda look diffuse, several issues have emerged over the years as women's core concerns (see Figure 1.1).

Rights Though the Universal Declaration of Human Rights, adopted by the United Nations nearly fifty years ago, recognized women's rights as an integral part of human rights, in many countries women still do not enjoy equal legal rights. Guaranteeing women equal rights under the law, enforcing these, and raising women's consciousness about their rights became major issues on the women's agenda. The United Nations Convention on the Elimination of Discrimination Against Women (UNCEDAW) was a major step forward in setting international standards of gender equality. However, about a quarter of the world's states are still to ratify CEDAW, and some have ratified it with reservations. Monitoring the ratifications and implementation of CEDAW remains a major challenge for the future.

Entitlement Early in the Decade for Women, data from around the world indicated that gender inequalities in access to and control over productive resources – land, capital, information, training, technology, the market, and so on – disadvantaged women in the labour market; that when endowed and equipped with productive resources women

Figure 1.1 Women's Agenda

1. Rights
   - Legal equality
   - Enforcement
   - Awareness-raising

2. Entitlement
   - Access to and control over productive resources and services

3. Investment
   - Elimination of the gender gaps in human development
   - Support for gender needs

4. Voice
   - Decisionmaking
   - Women's visions of alternative development agenda

5. Poverty
   - Policy/programme interventions
   - Female-headed households

6. Reproductive Labour
   - Male sharing of responsibilities
   - Public/private sector provisioning of services

7. Security
   - Domestic violence and abuse
   - Violence and harassment in the public domain

8. Empowerment
   - Assertion of own agency

could increase their productivity and ensure greater returns on their labour. Institutional and legal reforms to guarantee women equal rights to inherit and own property, obtain credit and become members of producers' organizations have been a longstanding item on the women's agenda.

Investment Investing in women is yet another consistent demand. It has been repeatedly argued that gender inequalities in human development – that is, in education, health and nutrition – have limited women's well-being as well as their income-earning capacity; that public- and private-sector investment is called for to close the gender gap in human development. Resources are needed not only to improve girls' and women's access to education, training, healthcare and nutrition; they are also required to support a wide range of hitherto-neglected concerns that deserve priority attention – such as women's health, science and technical training for women, gender stereotyping of curricula, and so on.

Voice Ensuring the presence of women's voices in decisionmaking has been another persistent concern, as their absence results in a continued marginalization of gender issues in public discourse. Women need to participate not simply as passive beneficiaries: their involvement as decisionmakers is central to the direction of development. Women's organizations and movements have helped to strengthen the voice of women in articulating not merely narrow WID concerns but also their vision of a total development agenda.

Poverty The growing burden of poverty on women has been a long-standing concern of the women's movement. Early in the Decade, data from around the world indicated that women were shouldering a disproportionate burden of poverty, in part because of gender inequalities in entitlement, investment and power. The plight of female-headed households, often the poorest of the poor, emerged as a global phenomenon. Feminists from the South especially have highlighted poverty as a priority issue, calling for policy/programme interventions to eliminate poverty and address the special needs of female-headed households.

Reproductive labour From the beginning of the Decade for Women it became apparent that the gender division of labour prevailing in most societies has resulted in a greater responsibility on the part of women for unpaid reproductive work (such as care of children, the sick and the elderly; household maintenance; provision of basic needs), and this has limited their participation in paid productive work, and paid and unpaid community and public service. Women's movements have demanded that men assume greater responsibility for childcare and household maintenance, and pressed for stronger social policies to ensure changes in laws and the provisioning of public- and private-sector services which would relieve women's reproductive burden. It was argued that without such support women would increase their productive roles only at the cost of their health and leisure.

Security Security from war and violence has been yet another major concern of the women's movement. Violence is used as an instrument of oppression against women, limiting their rights and choices and creating obstacles to equal participation. Security emerged as a key issue on the women's agenda, particularly in the post-Nairobi decade. During this period women mobilized to demand security within the household as well as outside it: security from domestic violence and abuse; from assault, rape and sexual harassment in schools, the workplace and streets; and from war-related violence that results in mass rapes and dislocation of populations.

Empowerment Though organization and consciousness-raising have been on the women's agenda all along, self-empowerment gained salience as a critical strategy only in the last decade. Over the years, there has been gradual recognition that mere access to resources or provisioning of services is not adequate to challenge the root causes of gender inequality; that women need to assert their own agency, and only through self-empowerment can they aspire to break out of gender subordination.

In the last two decades, the women's movement has succeeded in creating common ground among women worldwide around the above set of core concerns. Common ground was created not through a mono-lithic feminist vision but through a process of exchange and negotiation among women's groups from North and South. At the first World Conference on Women in Mexico in 1975, where many of the feminists from North and South met for the first time, there were heated debates and sharp division of opinion – equality appeared to be the priority of the First World; peace of the Second; and development of the Third World. By the time the Nairobi World Conference on Women was held in 1985, the interlinkages and indivisibility of the three themes – equality, development and peace – became clear to the feminists of North and South. The many exchanges between North and South held during the Decade facilitated consensus-building. These dialogues recognized the differences in interests and priorities between North and South, but at the same time they sought to build North–South alliances around common goals. Gender equality and social transformation emerged as two common objectives shared by many feminists from both North and South.

PERSPECTIVES FROM THE SOUTH

From the beginning of the Decade for Women, feminists from the South consistently articulated three major concerns. First, they underscored the need to link gender-, class- and race-based inequalities and discrimination, and argued that struggles against gender inequality must be accompanied by struggles against other forms of inequality and discrimination. Second, Southern feminists pointed out that to explain gender inequality, it was necessary to look at social structures, development paradigms and macro-policies rather than simply addressing social norms and cultures and WID-focused policies. They emphasized that an improvement in women's lives and opportunities is only possible through structural changes and changes in the macro-policy environment. Third, Southern feminists demanded not simply gender parity or gender balance in representation, but a total transformation of the development agenda from a gender perspective, elaborating a feminist vision of alternative development.

The holistic view of development envisioned by the Southern feminists has been reiterated in many major conferences and publications throughout the last twenty years. For example, in a regional South and Southeast Asian Conference held in Bangladesh in 1977, the participants demanded gender equality in 'the opportunities of development and in the decisionmaking processes' as well as women's involvement 'in all spheres of life in the processes of social and economic transformation'.[4] They declared that 'no amount of special programmes will succeed in integrating half the population of the country'.[5] In 1979 a position paper on feminist ideology published by the Asia Pacific Centre for Women and Development (APCWD) asserted that 'oppression of women is rooted in both inequalities and discrimination based on sex and in poverty and the injustice of the political and economic systems based on race and class'.[6] In 1982, the Dakar Declaration on Another Development with Women, drawn up by a group of African women, stated that:

> the most fundamental and underlying principle of Another Development should be that of structural transformation, a notion which challenges the economic, political and cultural forms of domination ... which are found at the international, national and household levels. Accordingly, at the international levels, Another Development should replace the forms of dependent development and unequal terms of exchange with that of mutually beneficial and negotiated interdependence.... Nationally, models of development have to be based on the principle of self reliance ... and the building of genuinely democratic institutions and practices.... At the local and household levels, the vision of Another Development ought to reject existing structures that create or reinforce a sexual division of labour.[7]

In 1985, putting forward a Third World women's perspective of development, DAWN – a network of Southern feminists – argued that:

> both poverty and gender subordination must be transformed by our vision ...
> in a world and in countries riven with differences of economic interest and
> political power, we cannot expect political will for systemic change to emerge
> voluntarily.... It must be fostered by mass movements that give central focus
> to the 'basic rights' of the poor and demand reorientation of policies, pro-
> grammes and projects toward that end.... The transformation of the structures
> of subordination that have been so inimical to women is the other part of our
> vision.... Changes in laws, civil codes, systems of property rights, control
> over our bodies, labour codes and the social and legal institutions that under-
> write male control and privilege are essential if women are to attain justice in
> society.[8]

What were the responses of the international donor agencies to the
demands of the women's movement, especially the concerns articulated
by the Southern feminists? Did the donors come forward with a
systematic response? Did they address the issues raised by the Southern
feminists?

THE DONORS' RESPONSE

The donors responded gradually and slowly. The issues brought forward by the women's movement were novel, and they were also critical
of donors' past policies. The criticisms came from several different
angles. Some, especially many of the earlier feminists from the North,
reproached the donors for past neglect and argued that what women
needed was more 'integration' – greater visibility, more participation,
additional resources, and so on.[9] Others, however, especially feminists
from the South, argued that it was not the lack of integration but the
exploitation and unequal conditions under which women were being
integrated in the production process that had caused gender inequalities;
that their greater integration in the prevailing development strategies
would only exacerbate the inequalities. What women needed was not
integration but a fundamental reorientation of existing development
paradigms.[10]

The donors were initially responsive to the integrationist perspective.
Instead of changing policy, programme and investment priorities, they
took an 'add-on' integrationist approach – adding a few specific
measures, and WID staff and projects. The institutionalization of WID,
rather than its operationalization, became a priority concern. Donors
spent the greater part of the Decade for Women advocating the adoption
of WID mandates, policies and measures. In 1983, the Development

Assistance Committee (DAC) of the Organization for Economic Co-operation and Development (OECD) adopted a set of WID Guiding Principles, which for the first time attempted to systematize and coordinate the response of bilateral donors. The DAC/WID Guiding Principles, which were later revised in 1989 in the light of the 1985 Forward Looking Strategies, endorsed 'integration' as the objective and urged DAC member donor organizations to adopt a series of measures grouped under four categories: (a) mandates, policy guidelines, and plans of action; (b) administrative measures; (c) implementation; and (d) coordination, consultation, and development education. The Guiding Principles, which were regularly monitored by the DAC Expert Group on WID, not only facilitated institutionalization of WID in bilateral donors agencies, they also influenced their institutionalization in multilateral agencies.[11]

The post-Nairobi decade witnessed a significant increase in donors' commitment to and resourcing of WID. Most agencies adopted WID policies and measures, and introduced various procedures to ensure agency compliance with WID mandates. Staffing and budgetary resources for WID were increased. Donors also started paying greater attention to operational issues, designing operational guidelines and tools and beginning to use macroeconomic policy frameworks and policy dialogues to address gender issues. Some of the initial approaches also came under review. For example, several agencies substituted other goals for the objective of 'integration' – for example, 'mainstreaming', or 'women's autonomy'. Similarly, many agencies changed the nomenclature of their programmes from 'Women in Development' (WID) to 'Gender and Development' (GAD), arguing that while WID focused primarily on women, a gender approach, by focusing on the socially constructed roles of both women and men, looks at women in the context of society and was better suited to cross-sectoral analysis.[12]

This greater attention and the increased resources resulted in a significant growth of WID/GAD-related activities both in donor agencies and in their partner countries, especially in the first few years after Nairobi. But by the early 1990s there were clear signs that the donors were losing their post-Nairobi euphoria. Several agencies reorganized their WID offices and cut back resources. Many within agencies started to talk about 'WID fatigue';[13] some donor assessments found WID losing 'momentum';[14] while still others pointed out that WID efforts were falling short of donors' lofty goals.[15] Donors began to talk about 'WID results' and 'measurable progress'.

What might explain this rapid rise of WID fatigue within the relatively short time span of half a decade? If donors and their development partners were able to stay with other issues such as population and

Figure 1.2 Analytical Framework for Assessment of WID/GAD Policies and Measures

1. Objective

   (A) Substantive
   - Women's advancement
   - Gender equality
   - Women's empowerment

   (B) Instrumental
   - Integration
   - Mainstreaming

2. Approach
   - Integrationist
   - Agenda-setting

3. Strategies

   (A) Institutional
   - Responsibility
   - Accountability
   - Coordination
   - Monitoring
   - Evaluation
   - Personnel policy

   (B) Operational
   - Guidelines
   - Training
   - Research
   - Special projects
   - Analytical tools
   - Country programming
   - Macro-policies
   - Policy dialogues

4. Measures of Progress

   (A) Mainstreaming
   - Resources
   - Discourse

   (B) Gender Equality
   - Law and norms
   - Human development

   (C) Empowerment
   - Women's movement
   - Public action
   - Decisionmaking

poverty alleviation for several decades with incremental results, why did they start becoming impatient with WID results? Is WID being judged differently from other issues? Or is there still no clear indicator to assess its performance and progress? Are donor agencies shifting attention to more fashionable issues? Or are donors simply tired, faced with too many mandates and too many countries, and coming to realize their role in influencing the process of development is limited? There are many unexplored issues that a systematic assessment of WID needs to address.

THE ANALYTICAL FRAMEWORK

This study has a relatively narrow focus: it looks at the experiences of four donor agencies and two of their partner countries over the last two decades and asks three basic sets of questions. First, what were the articulated objectives of their WID policies and measures? Were they responsive to the aspirations of the women's movement, particularly concerns raised by the feminists from the South? Was there a congruence between the objectives of the donors and those of their development partners? Second, did the donors and their partners adopt any identifiable set of strategies to realize the policy objectives? Were they effective? What were their implementation experiences? Finally, what were the results? Did the donors and their partners establish any indicator to assess achievement of goals? Was there any quantitative and qualitative evidence to suggest progress? What should be the measures of progress?

I use a relatively simple analytical framework to conceptualize and compare the policy objectives, strategies, and measures of progress (see Figure 1.2). To compare policy objectives I differentiate between substantive and process-focused instrumental objectives. In their various policy statements and documents donors have referred to substantive objectives such as women's advancement, gender equality, women's empowerment and so on. They have also committed themselves to process-focused instrumental objectives such as women's 'integration' and 'mainstreaming'. Generally, donors have highlighted process-focused instrumental objectives. Early on in the Decade, donors chose 'integration' as the objective of their policies. Agency documents referred to women's 'integration as agents and beneficiaries of development' or as 'full partners of men'. But, as noted earlier, many feminists, especially those from the South, rejected the goal of integration. They argued that women did not want to be integrated in an unequal and exploitative system – they wanted to change the prevailing system.

Dissatisfaction with the concept of integration led many development agencies and their partner countries to shift to a new term – 'mainstreaming' women in development. Mainstreaming was chosen as a goal because it was felt that during the Decade for Women, special WID ghettos were being created in the name of integration. But again, like the earlier objective of integration, mainstreaming was a catch-all term, and donors did not explain the reasons for their shift from integration to mainstreaming.

Mainstreaming: integrationist and agenda-setting

What does mainstreaming mean? How is it different from the earlier goal of integration? English-language dictionaries variously define 'mainstream' as 'the prevailing current, direction of activity/influence'[16] or 'the principal, dominant course, tendency or trend'.[17] Mainstreaming as a concept obviously reflects a desire for women to be at centre-stage, part of the mainstream. But how would women become part of the mainstream? In a paper commissioned by the OECD/DAC's Expert Group on WID to elaborate the concept of mainstreaming, I identified two broad approaches.[18] The first, 'integrationist', approach builds gender issues within existing development paradigms. Widening women-and-gender concerns across a broad spectrum of sectors is the key strategy within this concept: the overall development agenda is not transformed, but each issue is adapted to take into account women-and-gender concerns. A good example of the 'integrationist' approach is the practice of designing WID 'components' in major sectoral programmes and projects. Women are 'fitted' into as many sectors and programmes as possible, but sector and programme priorities do not change because of gender considerations.

The second approach, which I call 'agenda-setting', implies the transformation of the existing development agenda with a gender perspective. The participation of women as decisionmakers in determining development priorities is the key strategy here: women participate in all development decisions, and through this process bring about a fundamental change in the existing development paradigm. Women not only become a part of the mainstream, they also reorient the nature of the mainstream. It is not simply women as individuals but women's 'agenda' which gets recognition from the mainstream. An example of an agenda-setting approach is the prioritizing of women's empowerment in population sector programmes.

WID strategies: institutional and operational

In comparing WID strategies, two broad categories are again used: institutional and operational. Institutional strategies are the input-side interventions which aim primarily at structural changes within agencies and governments to facilitate the implementation of WID policies and measures. Instruments and procedures relating to WID/GAD responsibility, accountability, coordination, monitoring, evaluation, and personnel policy fall under the category of institutional strategies. Operational strategies, on the other hand, are the output-oriented measures designed to bring about a change in the work programmes of agencies and governments. Guidelines, training, research, special projects, analytical tools, country programming, macro-policies and policy dialogue are some of the operational strategies promoted so far.

Measuring progress

To assess progress towards goal achievement broad indicators are used. Since a great deal of donor agency effort was spent in achieving the goals of integration and/or mainstreaming, two rough indicators are constructed to gauge progress in mainstreaming. The first, mainstreaming resources, uses quantitative data, available in donor agencies and their counterpart governments, about women's representation on the staff and women-oriented assistance. It essentially measures agency and government input. The second indicator is primarily based on qualitative information. Key agency and government documents are analysed to assess achievements over time in mainstreaming gender issues in development discourse. It is oriented towards agencies' and the governments' output. To assess progress in achieving the two major goals of the women's movement – gender equality and women's empowerment – again rough indicators are constructed. Available data on human development and legal and institutional reforms from the two partner countries are used to underscore the kinds of progress that aid-recipient women have made in achieving gender equality. And both quantitative and qualitative data from the two partner countries are used to indicate whether women are being empowered. Since empowerment is a rather nebulous concept I use three main criteria – strengthening of the women's movement; participation in public action; and involvement in national and local decisionmaking bodies – to assess progress in empowerment.

Donors and their development partners

This study reviews and compares the experiences of four donors – the Canadian International Development Agency (CIDA); the Norwegian Agency for Development Cooperation (NORAD); the United Nations

Development Programme (UNDP); and the World Bank (WB) – and two development partner countries: Tanzania and Bangladesh.

The two bilateral donors – CIDA and NORAD – were selected because among donors they have a reputation of mounting major WID efforts. They number among the few agencies who had adopted detailed WID policies and plans before the end of the Decade. They also undertook their own internal assessments. In contrast, the two multilateral donors – UNDP and the World Bank – were chosen not on the strength of their WID mandates and policies, but because of the influence they wield in shaping the development strategies of the countries of the South. The World Bank through its conditionalities often dictates policy reforms to aid-recipient governments. The UNDP, as the largest fund, has a big presence within the United Nations system. The actions of these two agencies – what they advocate and what they omit or marginalize – have a strong impact on the policy analysis and investment decision of the aid-recipient countries.

The major consideration in selecting the two countries, Tanzania and Bangladesh, is the presence in them of a large number of donors, which make them an interesting case study of donor influence and the results of WID policies in two different continents. My own familiarity with these two countries (especially with my own country, Bangladesh) is another consideration that weighed heavily in the selection of the countries.

Although in making a comparison between the agencies and the countries I have drawn a number of conclusions about their commonalities and differences, it should be made clear that the agencies and the countries do not constitute a representative sample. For example, of the twenty-two DAC member donor organizations, the two reviewed by this study – CIDA and NORAD – are among those which have mounted the most WID efforts: many bilateral donors have only just started to take WID/GAD initiatives.[19]

DATA

This study is primarily based on published and unpublished data collected from the four donor agencies and the two national governments during 1991–92. Staff of donor agencies were interviewed both in the headquarters and in the field offices of Tanzania and Bangladesh. Government officials as well as women and men outside the government were interviewed in the two countries.

A great deal of data is available from agency and government sources about the extent to which they have adopted WID measures, but information about the impact of these measures on operations and on people on the ground is rather more limited. Operational and impact data are less systematic and precise. Until now, donors and governments have primarily monitored their WID activities, but not their results. A few agencies have attempted to evaluate their WID efforts; but of the four donors studied here, only CIDA has undertaken any systematic assessment of its WID policies.[20] Recently many agencies have started to evaluate their WID efforts as part of their preparation for the fourth World Conference on Women (WCW) in Beijing. OECD/DAC has completed a major assessment of DAC donors' WID efforts.[21]

The donors' assessment of effectiveness has been based mainly on the perceptions of their own staff; the views of the women who are the recipients of aid, on the receiving end of policies, were rarely solicited. However, the perceptions of agency staff varied a great deal, and I was particularly struck by the sharp contrast between the views expressed by the WID staff and those of the other agency staff. While the former were often critical of their agencies, the latter appeared to be generally complimentary about agency efforts and achievements.

The contrasting perspectives of the various people involved and the uneven quality of data make the assessment of WID measures difficult. Donors and governments have yet to collate and systematize the diverse information they have generated in the field. Researchers and activists outside the agencies generally do not have access to agency data and documents, and this has resulted in an information gap. By synthesizing information available from the various donor agencies and governments, this study attempts to fill the gap, and initiate a debate about past efforts and achievements as well as future challenges.

ORGANIZATION OF THIS STUDY

This book is divided into seven chapters. Following on from this introductory chapter, Chapter 2 looks at policy objectives and advocates. Based on a comparative review of the policy statements of donors and their development partners, it attempts to analyse and compare policy objectives, and to highlight common patterns and approaches. It investigates whether policies have attempted to address the agenda of the women themselves, especially the concerns of the Southern feminists. The chapter also briefly describes the policy advocates: the main players who influenced the adoption of the policies in different agencies and countries.

Chapters 3 and 4 describe the WID/GAD strategies adopted by the donors and their development partners. Chapter 3 focuses on institutional strategies, whereas Chapter 4 goes on to discuss operational strategies. Published and unpublished data and personal interviews are used to describe the implementation of strategies and to assess their efficacy, making a comparison between the efforts of the various donors and counterparts.

Chapter 5 attempts to assess results. Based on the available quantitative and qualitative data, it constructs several indicators to measure progress in achieving three major goals – mainstreaming, gender equality and women's empowerment. To a limited extent the donor agencies are already monitoring their mainstreaming efforts to increase women's share of agency staff and budget, and have also deliberately attempted to mainstream discussion of gender issues in agency documents. In contrast, the donor agencies have not made much effort systematically to monitor the achievements in gender equality and women's empowerment. The indicators used in this study to assess progress in achieving gender equality and women's empowerment suggest the kinds of tools donors and governments might use to assess the results of their WID measures. Chapter 6 summarizes the major findings of the study, highlighting both achievements and shortfalls, and identifying priority areas of action for the future. The final chapter pulls together the major conclusions of the study.

Throughout the study I generally use the term 'development partner', rather than 'aid recipient', to underscore the perspective we need to use in future. References to 'donors' and 'development partners' generally imply the four donors and two partners reviewed in the book. The terms WID/GAD are used to indicate changes in the nomenclature of the programmes.

NOTES

1. United Nations, *World Survey on the Role of Women in Development*, New York 1989, p. 5.

2. United Nations, *World Plan of Action for the Implementation of the Objectives of the International Women's Year*, New York 1975.

3. United Nations, *The Nairobi Forward Looking Strategies for the Advancement of Women*, New York 1986.

4. Rounaq Jahan and Hanna Papanek, eds., *Women and Development: Perspectives from South and South East Asia*, Bangladesh Institute of Law and International Affairs, Dhaka 1979, p. 11.

5. Ibid., p. 12.

6. APCWD, 'Report of the International Workshop on Feminist Ideology and Structures in the First Half of the Decade for Women', Bangkok, 20–24 June 1979, quoted in C. Bunch and R. Carillo, 'Feminist Perspectives on Women in Development', in Irene Tinker, ed., *Persistent Inequalities*, Oxford University Press, New York 1990, p. 77.

7. AAWORD/DHF, 'The Dakar Declaration on Another Development with Women: Development Dialogue', 1982, quoted in Bunch and Carillo, 'Feminist Perspectives', p. 79.

8. Gita Sen and Caren Grown, *Development, Crises and Alternative Visions: Third World Women's Perspectives*, Monthly Review Press, New York 1987, pp. 80–81.

9. Ester Boserup, *Women's Role in Economic Development*, St Martin's Press, New York 1970; Irene Tinker and Michelle B. Bramsen, eds., *Women and World Development*, ODC, Washington DC 1976.

10. Beneria Lourdes, ed., *Women and Development: The Sexual Division of Labour in Rural Societies*, Praeger, New York 1982; Kate Young, Carol Wolkowitz and Roslyn McCullagh, *Of Marriage and the Market*, Routledge, London 1984; Sen and Grown, *Development, Crisis and Alternative Visions*; Bunch and Carillo, 'Feminist Perspectives'; Geartje Lycklama, 'The Fallacy of Integration: The UN Strategy of Integrating Women into Development Revisited', paper presented for development policy seminar for UNDP staff, The Hague, November 1987.

11. Rounaq Jahan, *Assessment of Policies and Organizational Measures in Women in Development Adopted by DAC Member Countries: Theme 2 of the Assessment of WID Policies and Programs of DAC Members*, Directorate for Development Co-operation and Humanitarian Aid, Switzerland, and the United States Agency for International Development, 1994.

12. Caroline O.N. Moser, *Gender Planning and Development*, Routledge, London 1993.

13. Personal interviews in OECD, NORAD, and CIDA, 1991.

14. CIDA, *Gender as a Cross Cutting Theme in Development Assistance – An Evaluation of CIDA's WID Policy and Activities, 1984–1992*, Executive Summary, July 1993, p. 4.

15. UNDP, 'Women in Development: Report of the Administrator', 30 April 1990.

16. *Webster's New World Dictionary*, Second Concise Edition, Simon and Schuster, New York 1982.

17. *Dictionary of the English Language*, Random House, New York 1968.

18. Rounaq Jahan, 'Mainstreaming Women in Development in Different Settings', paper presented at a seminar on Mainstreaming Women in Development organized by the OECD/DAC/WID Expert Group, Paris, 18–19 May 1992.

19. Rounaq Jahan, *Assessment of Policies and Organizational Measures in Women in Development*.

20. CIDA, *Gender as a Cross Cutting Theme in Development Assistance*.

21. Ria Brouwers, *Review of the Integration of Gender Concerns in the Work of DAC: Theme 1 of the Assessment of WID Policies and Programs of DAC Members*, The Hague, the Netherlands, Directorate General for International Cooperation of the Netherlands, 1993; Rounaq Jahan, *Assessment of Policies and Organizational Measures in Women in Development*; and Julia Z. Paton, *WID as a Cross-Cutting Issue in Development Aid Evaluations: Theme 3 Synthesis: Summary and Conclusions*, CIDA, Ottawa 1994.

CHAPTER 2

POLICY OBJECTIVES
AND ADVOCATES

Early in the Decade the equity principle had been made even more persuasive by its linkage with utility principle. Women had been a missing link in development, now they were being found: they could actually be a valuable resource, indeed were half, or more, of a nation's human resources, no longer to be wasted.... The prospect of steering women from the margin to the mainstream was as exciting to some would be developers as to female recipients of such policies and programmes. 'Women in Development' became the Decade's overnight catchphrase, a seductive one, which for a time, at least, could evade the question of what kind of development women were to be drawn into.

> Lucille M. Mair, 'Women: A Decade is Time Enough',
> *Third World Quarterly*, vol. 8, no. 2, 1986, pp. 586–7

OBJECTIVES AND APPROACHES

Did the donors and their partner governments clearly establish a set of objectives when they initiated their WID policies and actions? Did these reflect the concerns of the women's movement? Did the policy objectives and approaches change over the years? Were there any discernible patterns?

Donors and their partner countries varied in their articulation of policy objectives for women. The two bilateral donors, NORAD and CIDA, spelled out their objectives in some detail when they adopted their WID policies. In contrast, the two multilateral donors did not elaborate or even adopt formal WID policies for a long time, and started implementing WID measures before adopting formal policy documents. The two countries, Tanzania and Bangladesh, also initiated WID activities before formulating official policies on women. However, even in situations where formal policies were missing, the official documents of the agencies and governments did pursue objectives of taking WID measures.

Figure 2.1   Policy Objectives, Approaches and Methodologies

1. Objectives

    (A) Substantive

    • Women's advancement
    • Gender equality
    • Women's empowerment

    (B) Instrumental

    • Integration
    • Mainstreaming

2. Approaches

    • Integrationist
    • Agenda-setting

3. Methodologies

    • Women in development (WID)
    • Gender and development (GAD)
    • WID-specific
    • WID-integrated

Common patterns

Over the years the articulation of policy objectives has changed, in ways which are common to the various donors (see Figure 2.1). Prior to the Decade for Women – in the 1950s and 1960s – the emphasis was on substantive objectives. Women's welfare and women's advancement were the two most frequently cited objectives. During the Decade, when the economic role of women was suddenly discovered and special machineries were created to promote women's advancement, process-focused instrumental objectives took precedence over substantive objectives. 'Integration of women in development' emerged as the most common objective. By the end of the Decade many agencies and governments had started embracing another instrumental objective – mainstreaming women in development. Substantive common objectives were also noted – women's advancement, gender equality, and women's empowerment.

In the last two decades, the approaches of WID policies have also gradually changed. Early in the Decade, the emphasis was on an integrationist approach. Attempts were made to find and add on WID issues in each sector. As a result, gender issues were discovered in a wide variety of economic sectors. But the feminist demand to transform the development agenda through a gender lens slowly led agencies to turn to an agenda-setting approach. In the post-Nairobi decade, agencies increasingly embraced the approaches advocated by the women's movement. Women's empowerment has found a place in the agency documents.

As noted earlier, many agencies also shifted their methodological approaches from 'women in development' (WID) to 'gender and development' (GAD), the former implying a consideration of women's roles only and the latter paying attention to the socially constructed roles of both women and men. Agencies and governments also changed their focus from 'WID-specific' to 'WID-integrated' activities, signifying a change from limiting projects to women to addressing gender issues in general development programmes and projects.

Though feminists in the women's movement underscored the conceptual differences between the different policy goals, approaches and methodologies, and advocated pursuit of a coherent set, the practitioners within agencies advocated a combined approach.[1] For example, donors often simultaneously articulated substantive and instrumental objectives and integrationist and agenda-setting mainstreaming approaches. They used both WID and GAD methodologies. They implemented WID-specific as well as WID-integrated activities.

The simultaneous pursuit of different policy goals, approaches and methods often created confusion and contradictory trends. But donors pointed out that a combined approach was best suited to serve their various needs and constituencies. The donors argued that they needed to emphasize instrumental goals over substantive ones, as WID had to be first institutionalized in agencies before it could aspire to influence operations. They stressed that both integrationist and agenda-setting approaches were necessary – that integration is needed to set the agenda, and that women needed to be part of the mainstream in order to change it. And they underscored the necessity of carrying out both 'WID-specific' and 'WID-integrated' activities, stressing that in some situations – such as institution-building or pilot innovations – a 'WID-specific' approach was necessary; while in others – such as sector programmes – WID-integrated methods were more appropriate. Similarly, many agencies followed GAD methodology for project analysis and identification, but WID focus for project activities.

Within the broad framework of common patterns there were, however, considerable differences between the four donors, and the two countries.

NORAD

Norway's WID policy goals have changed over the past three decades from a straightforward emphasis on women's welfare to an amalgam of women's welfare, integration and mainstreaming. For example, parliamentary White Paper no. 29 (1971–72), which for the first time raised the question of women's issues, called for improvement of women's weak social position. In contrast, parliamentary White Paper no. 96 (1974–75) urged women's active integration in development, but still addressed women's issues in the narrow context of health and social welfare programmes. The 1984–85 parliamentary White Paper gave a more comprehensive WID mandate: it recognized women's productive as well as reproductive roles, made WID a priority objective of aid and tied WID up with the overall objectives of development assistance.

Norway's WID policy – set in 1985 – clearly endorsed an agenda-setting mainstreaming objective. It called for 'placing women in the mainstream of development' as well as changing the mainstream 'to make it benefit women'. The policy underscored the importance of building on 'women's strength, needs and interests', urging a stronger focus on the 'human and social aspects of development' as well as 'reconceptualization' of some aspects of 'the economic and organizational models on which traditional development strategies are based'.[2]

The 1985 WID policy and the Action Plan – which is still to be revised – established two main goals and six sub-goals. The two main goals were: (1) 'women's living and working conditions must be improved'; and (2) 'women must be motivated and provided with opportunities to participate in economic, cultural and political activities with a view to changing the mainstream of development to make it benefit women'. The six sub-goals listed a core feminist agenda: securing rights; gaining access to and control over resources; increasing productivity and returns on labour; sharing childcare responsibilities; and improving health, living and working conditions. Compared to most other donors of the time, who still emphasized WID integration, Norway came forward with a clearly enunciated agenda which set mainstreaming objectives.

NORAD funded both WID-specific and WID-integrated activities. In Tanzania and Bangladesh it backed up the activities of the ministries for women, and also supported women-specific research and field projects out of its WID funds. At the same time NORAD funded WID-integrated activities in its rural development programmes in Tanzania and Bangladesh. Although it continued to call its programme 'WID', NORAD introduced gender-analysis methodologies, especially in its training programmes. The agenda-setting approach has enabled NORAD to emphasize the objective of women's empowerment. It has provided direct support to women's organizations in partner countries.

CIDA

Following an overall national policy to achieve gender equality, CIDA announced a WID policy for the first time in 1976. It declared five guidelines, but had no action plan or timetable to achieve these objectives. In 1984, CIDA adopted a more detailed WID policy framework, and in 1986 a five-year WID action plan. In 1992, CIDA came forward with a revised WID policy framework. The successive formulations show the gradual evolution of policy objectives and approaches in CIDA.

The 1976 WID policy guidelines emphasized women's equal participation as agents and beneficiaries, and their 'equitable integration into the mainstream of the agency's work'.[3] The 1984 WID policy pledged that 'the full range of its development assistance will contribute substantively to the realization of the full potential of women as agents and beneficiaries of the development process'. CIDA's role was defined as being responsive to the 'development objectives of third world women by supporting their ... initiatives to improve their situation'.[4] However, it maintained a focus on the integrationist approach. Unlike that of NORAD, CIDA's WID policy did not refer to any specific feminist agenda. Its seven policy objectives talked generally of increasing women's participation in development interventions, including women in CIDA programmes, raising awareness about women's multiple roles, closing the economic gap between women and men, and generating income for women. The revised WID interim policy of 1992 emphasized women's decisionmaking roles, as opposed to their roles as agents and beneficiaries of development, thereby indicating a growing sensitivity towards an agenda-setting approach. It underscored the need for CIDA to work towards the 'empowerment of women'.[5] The major goal of CIDA's revised WID policy was stated to be ensuring 'the full participation of women as equal partners in the sustainable development of their societies'.[6] The four specific objectives included elimination of discriminatory barriers against women, promotion of women's human rights, and building the institutional capacities of CIDA, as well as its development partners, to integrate fully gender considerations in their work.

The evolution of CIDA's WID policy statements from 1976 to 1992 thus indicates a gradual progression from women's 'integration as agents and beneficiaries' to women's 'empowerment' as 'decisionmakers'. Over the years, CIDA shifted from a WID to a mixed WID/GAD approach.

The 1984 policy was called WID, but the revised policy in 1992 was termed 'Women in Development and Gender Equity'.[7] Like NORAD, CIDA supported both WID-specific and WID-integrated activities. For example, in Bangladesh in the bilateral country programme CIDA supported mainly WID-integrated activities; WID-specific research and projects were generally supported out of NGO and Canada funds. Again, as with NORAD, empowerment approaches were limited to CIDA support of NGO activities.

UNDP

Though UNDP issued WID project and programming guidelines in 1976 and 1977 respectively, a formal WID policy was articulated only in 1987. The 1976 and 1977 guidelines perceived women as a 'disadvantaged' group needing 'special consideration',[8] but UNDP also acknowledged that women's roles affect 'the full spectrum of societal activities', and that 'corrective measures' to integrate women would require 'reallocation of resources across the board'.[9]

UNDP's 1987 WID policy statement was brief. The agency stated its concern as ensuring 'the integration of women as participants and beneficiaries in all of its development programme and projects'.[10] The policy statement did not pledge gender equity, nor did it identify any feminist agenda. Instead it emphasized country-specific contexts and promised simply a 'larger role for women'. In recent years, UNDP has started to refer to 'mainstreaming'. It has also highlighted national capacity-building as a priority objective. In some countries, such as Bangladesh, UNDP documents have started to refer to the goal of women's empowerment.[11]

Starting with a WID approach, UNDP officially shifted to GAD in 1992. Its WID division was dismantled and a GAD programme was created which was mandated to work collaboratively with the other priority themes of UNDP. Like NORAD and CIDA, UNDP supported both WID-specific and WID-integrated activities, the latter being primarily WID components in sector programmes. However, compared to the two bilateral donors, UNDP was much less active in the field of WID in Tanzania and Bangladesh.

The World Bank

The World Bank came forward with a policy paper on women only in 1994, though it established a WID-responsible office nearly twenty years earlier. Like UNDP, the bank referred to a broad objective: 'enhancing women's participation in economic development'.[12] The Bank's substantive policy objectives have not changed much since 1987, when its operative WID policy statement called for 'enhancing the role of women in economic development'.[13]

The 1994 policy paper, however, underscored shifts in the Bank's instrumental objectives and approaches. It has committed itself to 'mainstreaming gender concerns into its operations' and stated that its analytical framework would change from WID to GAD; changing male roles and responsibilities is also explicitly recognized. The approach is, however, primarily integrationist. The policy paper addresses three issues on the women's agenda: poverty, entitlement and investment. Women's development is justified on the grounds of social justice and poverty alleviation as well as economic growth.[14]

The rationale for promoting women's participation has not varied significantly between 1987 and 1994. The 1994 policy paper justifies investment in women to promote growth, efficiency and sustainable development, reduce poverty, slow population growth rates and improve child survival and overall family health.[15] The 1988 annual report of the Bank also talked about 'including women in development' to attain other development objectives – economic growth, efficient and sustainable utilization of resources, alleviation of poverty, improved family welfare and slower population growth.[16] The 1990 and 1991 annual reports of the Bank similarly referred to economic performance, poverty reduction, slower population growth and environmental sustainability.

In the two partner countries, the World Bank has gradually shifted its support from WID-specific activities to WID components in major sector programmes. In Bangladesh, for example, it has taken a 'package approach' in education-sector assistance.[17]

Tanzania

The 1967 Arusha Declaration in Tanzania, which forms the political foundation of the country, emphasized socialism and self-reliance, democracy and human equality, and endorsed the principles of gender equity and women's equal legal rights. The government of Tanzania also recognized the need to take proactive measures to close the existing gender gap. Separate women's organizations and special women's quotas in the various political bodies, including the National Assembly, were identified as specific instruments to promote women's participation in politics. The policy of universal primary education encouraged girls' enrolment, and rules were relaxed to facilitate girls' access to higher education.

In 1988 Tanzania formulated a policy on women, finally adopted in 1993, which emphasized substantive objectives such as gender equality and women's advancement. It identified specific issues on the women's agenda such as guaranteeing women's equal legal rights, prohibiting discrimination, and ensuring political and economic participation through special quotas and through access to and control over productive resources. The policy also highlighted the need for social transformation, such as equal responsibilities of men and women in the family, and equal education and upbringing of boys and girls.[18] The country's economic development policies concentrate on similar areas of concern: legal rights; the reduction of women's workload; and an increase in access to education, training and work and employment opportunities, particularly in agriculture.[19]

The official documents in Tanzania thus stress gender equality as an objective; and legal and institutional reforms, and investment in human development, especially education, and political participation as the means to achieve this goal. The official statements refer neither to 'integration' nor 'mainstreaming' objectives, nor to 'WID' and 'GAD' approaches. Indeed, officials and non-officials interviewed in Tanzania argued that the debates surrounding these English-language terms had very little relevance for them, and that words such as 'gender' and 'mainstreaming' could not be easily translated into the national language, Swahili.

Bangladesh

Bangladesh has yet to formulate a policy on women. But the country's constitution guarantees women's equal rights (Article 28(1); 28(2); 28(3)). It also sanctions proactive measures in favour of women. Like that of Tanzania, the Bangladesh government has employed quotas to ensure women's participation in politics, introduced legal reforms to protect women from violence, and undertaken special measures to increase girls' enrolment in schools.

However, unlike Tanzania, in Bangladesh both officials and non-officials have followed closely the donors' vocabulary. The successive five-year-plan documents have articulated the official perspective of government WID objectives, and these have changed over the years following the trends established by the donors. For example, the first five-year plan (1973–78) did not specifically focus on women's roles in economic development, but singled them out only under the social welfare sector programme. The second five-year plan (1980–85) talked about women's development, but treated it as a special and separate issue, which was continued in the third five-year plan (1985–90). The fourth five-year plan (1990–95) for the first time used terms such as 'mainstream' and 'gender', and adopted 'bringing women in the mainstream of development planning' as an important strategy.[20] It established nine specific objectives for its WID policy, which included such concerns as increasing women's participation in public decisionmaking; raising productivity and income; improving nutrition and health; reducing population growth, infant and maternal mortality and the male–female literacy gap; and ensuring participation of the 'poorer 50 per cent' of women in development.[21]

Unlike Tanzania, which pledged gender equality in the socialization of the family, Bangladesh limited its objective to equality in the public domain. Though many NGOs in Bangladesh have been quite successful in demonstrating the efficacy of empowerment approaches, the official statements on women did not embrace the term.

The shifts in language – from welfare to integration to mainstreaming; from WID to GAD – have taken place in Bangladesh without much internal debate and discussion. Though many of these English-language terms are as difficult to translate into Bengali as into Swahili, officials and non-officials alike appear to have quickly adjusted to the changes initiated by donors, without debating the rationale behind these changes.

Women's development or women's vision of development?

How well do the donors' WID objectives reflect the goals of the women's movement, especially those of the South? As noted in Chapter 1, the women's movement in the South consistently put forward a vision not simply of women's development but of an alternative model of development where gender equality goes hand in hand with equality between classes, races and nations. The Southern feminists underscored the need to change the existing development models and practices which perpetuate different forms of inequality and exploitation. The objectives articulated by the donors, on the other hand, emphasized women's development with very little reference to a vision of alternative development. The donors highlighted gender equality but did not link it with success in other struggles for equality; they stressed integration and mainstreaming but did not criticize mainstream models and practices. Of the four donors, only NORAD appeared to be somewhat sensitive to the need for changing the mainstream: it called for reconceptualization of economic and organizational models. CIDA's 1992 WID policy statement, by establishing sustainable development as a goal, opened up the possibility of changing existing development paradigms and building on women's vision of alternative development.

How responsive have donors been to their partner governments? Did the donors' WID objectives represent the priorities established by their partners? Again it appears that donors tended to bypass a large part of their partners' agendas. For example, the governments of

Tanzania and Bangladesh emphasized three strategies to achieve gender equality – legal and institutional reforms, political participation, and access to and control over productive resources. But until recently donors focused primarily on the issue of productive resources. Donors' emphasis on development inputs often resulted in diverting their partners' attention from the critical issues of institutional and legal reforms and political action to the implementation of vocational training and income-generating projects. Only in the last few years have donors turned their attention from projects to policy and institutional concerns and started advocating legal and institutional reforms to entitle women to productive resources.

TARGETS

Who were the targets of the WID policies? Again, donors and their partner governments differed. For the donors, a major target was the agency itself. A lot of donor effort was directed at changing agency procedures and practices, and attitudes of agency staff. For example, CIDA and UNDP's WID policy-goal statements specifically referred to reforming agency procedures in order fully to integrate gender concerns. As will be discussed in Chapters 3 and 4, CIDA, NORAD and UNDP developed a variety of strategies to institutionalize WID within their agencies' procedures. In contrast, the World Bank spent less effort in changing the agency's internal processes and procedures. The Bank's efforts were more outward-oriented to the recipient governments.

The partner governments of Tanzania and Bangladesh were slow in coming forward with measures designed to change the whole government machinery. Their internal reform efforts were primarily restricted to establishing the national machineries. The machineries generally directed their focus outward towards women, especially implementing projects for women. They took less interest in changing government rules, procedures and policies in order to make them gender-responsive.

Although women in the aid-recipient countries were the major target of WID policies, the policy statements of both donors and their partners generally ignored the agency of the aid-recipient women. Only CIDA seemed to be somewhat sensitive to the issue. Its 1984 and 1992 policy statements talked about 'responding' to and 'supporting' the 'initiatives' of Third World women. Donors' policy statements also generally made very little reference to the role of partner governments. Only UNDP talked about country-specific contexts and the need to build national capacities. In recent years NORAD has also started to stress the responsibilities of aid recipients for their own development.[22] The World

Figure 2.2   Policy Advocates and Targets

1. Advocates

    (A) Insiders

    • Activists within agencies/governments
    • Special machineries/WID specialists
    • Corporate/state leadership

    (B) Outsiders

    • Women's organizations
    • Research/academic institutions
    • Civic and political organizations

2. Targets

    • Agency/government processes and procedures
    • Public policies/institutions
    • Women beneficiaries

Bank has also underscored the need to strengthen the institutional capacity in partner countries.[23]

Early in the Decade, projects were the preferred instrument for reaching the targets. The multilateral donors generally worked only with governments. The bilateral donors supported both government and non-government initiatives, funding a wide variety of projects including advocacy and capacity-building initiatives of women's groups and organizations. In contrast, the multilateral donors, especially the World Bank, tended to support projects in Bank-identified priority sectors, such as population and education. Only recently have some of the donors started to raise policy and institutional issues in their dialogue with the partner governments. This shift in emphasis from projects to policy was influenced by a general shift in the donors' mode of operations from project aid to policy and programmes assistance.

Donors chose different paths of WID action within their own agencies and in the aid-recipient countries. In their own agencies, donors took a step-by-step approach: pushing adoption of WID mandates and policies first, followed by the elaboration of administrative measures and design of operational tools, staff training and projects.[24] But in the partner countries, donors moved directly into field-based projects without first facilitating the development of national policies and institutional frameworks. The donors' emphasis on field projects in a policy and institutional vacuum often diverted the attention of the partner governments from their primary task of setting their own priorities and strategies. Instead of looking within their own country for successful approaches, they were reduced to being delivery mechanisms for donor-developed projects.

ADVOCATES

Who were the advocates of the WID policies? How did these policies come to be institutionalized within agencies and governments? Generally, an alliance of insiders and outsiders worked together to institutionalize the policies in the donor agencies and the partner governments. In the bilateral donor agencies, women's organizations and networks from the donor countries were the major outside influence. A few committed feminist staff within the agencies also played an important role, acting as catalysts to mobilize external forces. In the case of the multilateral agencies, powerful members of the governing boards – especially from the Nordic countries, Netherlands, the USA and Canada – together with inside feminist advocates and the top (male) leadership played an influential role in instituting WID measures. Women's lobby groups in donor countries were the major outside pressure group. In the partner countries, national machineries were the only inside advocates, and they were generally weak and ineffective. Women's organizations and the top (male) political leadership often worked as effective outside advocates. Donor agencies also were a major outside influence.

International networking facilitated the institutionalization of WID policies. Southern feminists were often invited to discuss gender issues before Northern audiences and the male decisionmakers of donor agencies. Similarly, feminists from the North and WID officials from donor agencies raised gender issues in dialogues with aid-recipient governments. The networking between feminists from donor agencies and those from partner countries proved to be a very effective strategy in institutionalizing WID measures in both donor agencies and partner countries.[25]

Though feminists and women's organizations from the partner countries played important advocacy roles in donor organizations and in international fora, they could not exert similar influence on their own governments. Feminists and autonomous women's organizations were small in number and they had limited political influence. In both Tanzania and Bangladesh, the governments established national women's organizations to mobilize women's political support. Instead of acting as the voice of the women to the government, these organizations tended to act as the governments' voice to the women. However, non-government women's organizations have increasingly gained in strength and begun to lobby their governments, parliaments and political parties. The governments, in turn, have also began to recognize the important role of the non-government organizations. The GO–NGO relationship, marked by suspicion and acrimony at the beginning of the Decade for Women, gradually became more cooperative.

Within donor agencies, feminists inside the bureaucracy reached out to outside feminists in the women's movement to work in alliance. This was particularly evident in the early years of the Decade for Women, when WID programmes did not achieve a foothold in the donor agencies. The insiders needed the political support of outsiders to strengthen their position within the bureaucracy. They also depended on outside expertise to advocate the issues. But as the WID programmes became institutionalized, insiders tended to turn back towards their own top management for support. They also gradually developed in-house WID/GAD expertise, and the ties with outside advocates, especially women's movements, became weak.

In the partner countries, the strategy of inside–outside feminist alliance was largely missing, and indeed there was often jealousy and animosity between the two groups. The number of women within the government was small in these countries, and the absence of a critical mass made the women insecure and reluctant to develop a strategy of alliance-building either inside or outside the government. National laws also discouraged such political strategies, as bureaucrats were expected to be non-political and non-partisan. In the absence of an inside–outside coalition, donors often stepped in to play a bridging role. The donors reached out to both the official and unofficial women's organizations, establishing forums where both official and NGO women could meet on an equal basis.

The insider–outsider alliance of advocacy worked better within the bilateral agencies than in the multilateral ones. The initial push for WID in both NORAD and CIDA came from women's organizations in these countries. In the case of Norway, a 'women's contact group' was established in 1973, consisting of representatives of several women's organizations and NORAD. The group met frequently and called for a thorough assessment of the impact of Norwegian development assistance on women. The pressure from the contact group led to more attention being focused on WID – such as the initiation of evaluations and studies to gauge the impact on women of Norwegian-assisted projects,[26] support to women-specific projects, and recruitment of a WID consultant in NORAD. In the case of CIDA, Canadian women's groups and CIDA co-sponsored a series of workshops across Canada in 1975 which recommended, among other things, the establishment of an advisory group to ensure that CIDA projects benefited women. As a follow-up to this, in 1976 CIDA announced a WID policy, created a responsibility structure for women and appointed a WID coordinator.

Though the alliance of inside–outside feminist advocates was important for both NORAD and CIDA, there were also differences between the two agencies. In NORAD, the inside advocates were generally young women in junior positions. The higher management and the agency as a whole were not involved in advocating WID or preparing the WID Plan of Action. In 1982, NORAD established a working group of six to draft the WID Plan of Action, which largely comprised young feminists. Though agency-wide input was solicited by the working group, since senior and junior management were not deeply involved, a feeling developed within NORAD that the WID Plan was the brainchild of a small group of feminists.[27]

In contrast, in CIDA there was stronger involvement of higher management and staff throughout the agency in drafting the WID policy framework and Plan of Action. There was strong support from CIDA's president, Margaret Catly-Carlson, who also happened to be a woman. The WID policy framework was developed by the senior-level President's Committee, which included the top management of CIDA. The same committee also developed a WID Plan of Action, but this was later discarded with the argument that the WID Implementation Plan should have institutional ownership and its drafting should involve the whole agency.[28] Accordingly a middle-level committee of all CIDA branches, chaired by the vice-president for policy, developed the WID Plan of Action, including sub-objectives, activities and responsibilities.

In the two multilateral organizations – the World Bank and the UNDP – inside–outside alliance was relatively weak. Women's organizations within the donor countries exerted some influence, but only indirectly through the governing boards. Women's movements and feminists from the South had very little access to the multilateral agencies, especially the World Bank. The major push for WID in these two agencies came at the end of the Decade for Women. In both, the main advocates were the governing board, particularly board-members from the donor countries, and the corporate heads – Barber Connable of the World Bank, William Draper of the UNDP. However, though at the UNDP and the World Bank top management pushed WID issues, no attempt was made to involve the whole agency in drafting a WID Policy and Action Plan, as there was at CIDA. WID policy formulation was left largely to the WID directorate in both the agencies. The agency as a whole did not have a sense of ownership of its WID policies.

In both of the multilateral agencies the pressure of board members from the donor countries – especially Western donors – was coupled with funding incentive from these countries for WID. This concentration of advocacy and funding support gave WID the image of being predominantly a 'donor's issue' in these agencies. The absence of networking with women's organizations from the South, and the relative lack of enthusiasm from Southern members of the governing board, further exacerbated this Western donor-driven image of WID. While the two bilateral donors effectively utilized the alliances of North–South women's networks to advocate gender issues, the multilateral agencies largely depended on an alliance between inside advocates and Western donor board-members.

In the partner countries, the inside advocates – the national machineries – lacked the perspective gained through building strategic alliances with non-governmental women's organizations and other government departments. The top decisionmakers within the government – the president or the prime minister – sometimes turned out to be strong WID advocates. Nyerere in Tanzania and Ziaur Rahman in Bangladesh were vocal advocates of women's advancement. This greatly facilitated the task of putting women on the development agenda of these countries. But the national governments in both countries failed to use the knowledge, expertise and commitment of their own feminists and autonomous women's organizations to optimum effect.

SUMMARY

Over the years, the articulation of policy objectives has changed – from women's advancement to gender equality and women's empowerment; from integration to mainstreaming women in development. Policy approaches also gradually evolved from being integrationist to agenda-setting. The methodological approaches shifted from 'women in development' to 'gender and development'. Projects moved from WID-specific to WID-integrated approaches. Donors and governments generally pursued different policy goals, approaches and methodologies simultaneously, arguing that a combined approach was necessary to serve their different needs and constituencies. But this introduced internal contradictions in the WID policy objectives and approaches. There were some marked differences between the donors and their partner governments. Donors highlighted the objectives of integration and mainstreaming; partners highlighted gender equality. Donors focused on giving women access to productive resources; partners prioritized legal and institutional reforms, political action and education for women. A major focus of the donors' WID policies was the agency itself, and changing internal processes and procedures was a dominant preoccupation. The policies of partners, on the other hand, were less concerned with changing their own machineries, and were primarily targeted at women.

In general, an alliance of insiders and outsiders worked together to institutionalize WID policies in agencies and governments. International networking between Northern and Southern feminists facilitated the process. The inside–outside alliance was stronger in the cases of bilateral donors than in multilateral agencies and the partner countries.

NOTES

1. Caroline O.N. Moser, *Gender Planning and Development: Theory, Practice and Training*, Routledge, London and New York 1993, pp. 130–32.

2. The Royal Norwegian Ministry of Development Cooperation, *Norway's Strategy for Assistance to Women in Development*, 1985, pp. 5–6.

3. CIDA, *CIDA's Women in Development Programme*, Evaluation Assessment Report, December 1990, Annex 2.

4. CIDA, *Women in Development: CIDA Action Plan*, 1986, p. 8.

5. CIDA, *Women in Development and Gender Equity*, Administrative Notice No. 92–26, 21 April 1992, p. 1.

6. Ibid.

7. Ibid.

8. UNDP, *Guidelines on Project Formulation*, 15 September 1976, and *Guidelines on the Integration of Women in Development*, 25 February 1977.

9. UNDP, *Guidelines on the Integration of Women in Development*, 25 February 1977.

10. UNDP, *Women in Development*, Policy and Procedures, 17 November 1987.

11. UNDP, *Women's Empowerment*, UNDP's 1994 *Report on Human Development in Bangladesh*, 1994.

12. The World Bank, *Enhancing Women's Participation in Economic Development*, 1994.

13. The World Bank, *Women in Development: A Progress Report on the World Bank Initiative*, 1990, p. 1.

14. The World Bank, *Enhancing Women's Participation in Economic Development*.

15. Ibid.

16. The World Bank, *Annual Report*, 1988, p. 44.

17. The World Bank, *Enhancing Women's Participation in Economic Development*.

18. Quoted in NORAD, *Action Plan for Women in Development*, Tanzania 1989.

19. Ibid.

20. Government of Bangladesh, *The Fourth Five-Year Plan*, 1990–95, pp. viii–2.

21. Ibid., pp. 1–9.

22. NORAD, *Strategies for Development Co-operation: NORAD in the 1990s*, Oslo, September 1990.

23. The World Bank, *Enhancing Women's Participation in Economic Development*.

24. Rounaq Jahan, *Assessment of Policies and Organizational Measures in Women in Development Adopted by DAC Member Countries: Theme 2 of the Assessment of WID*

Policies and Programs of DAC Members, Directorate for Development Co-operation and Humanitarian Aid, Switzerland, and the United States Agency for International Development, 1994.

25. Ibid.

26. Ragnhild Lund, *Evaluation of NORAD Projects and Effects on Women,* NORAD 1978; Karin Stoltenberg, *The Situation of Women in Developing Countries,* 1978.

27. Personal Interviews, NORAD, May 1991.

28. Personal Interview with Margaret Catly-Carlson, New York, March 1993.

CHAPTER 3

INSTITUTIONAL STRATEGIES

> Gender ideologies reduce the capability of organizations to realize their mandates, but offices that advocate change enhance that capability only slightly and only after herculean effort. When a gender advocacy office pursues bureaucratic politics through bargaining and constituency building, broad based alliances that prompt penetration of the procedural and technical core do not occur. Rather, such offices shoulder the burden themselves, with resulting polarization. The irony, then, is that while gender is the fundamental issue at stake, gender is counterproductive as an organizing tool.
>
> Kathleen Staudt, *Women, Foreign Assistance and Advocacy Administration*, New York 1985, p. 135.

In the last two decades, donor agencies and their partner governments have adopted a variety of measures designed to institutionalize WID/GAD in their organizations. These measures were detailed by the two bilateral donors in their five-year WID action plans. The two multilateral donors and the two countries, on the other hand, adopted various measures gradually, on an ad hoc basis. The institutional strategies included a variety of procedures relating to WID/GAD responsibility, accountability, coordination, monitoring, evaluation and personnel policies (see Figure 3.1). Not all donors and national governments adopted all of the instruments and procedures. However, each made an effort to take some measures to institutionalize WID. As pointed out in Chapter 1, it is difficult to assess the efficacy of the various institutional strategies because of a lack of systematic data about the actual workings of different measures. Still, enough information is available to identify some common patterns and draw a few conclusions.

RESPONSIBILITY

Prior to the Decade for Women, none of the donor agencies or their partner governments had any administrative structure specifically responsible for women's issues. WID gained a tentative institutional foothold only after the first UN Women's Conference in Mexico, which urged governments and international organizations to establish specific

Figure 3.1   Institutional Strategies

1. Responsibility

    (A) Structure
    • Advisory position
    • Administrative unit
    • Focal point

    (B) Function
    • Policy and strategy development
    • Advocacy, coordination and monitoring
    • Technical support for operations
    • Implementation

2. Accountability

    (A) Internal
    • Staff performance appraisal
    • Project/programme screening
    • Corporate/programme evaluation

    (B) Public
    • Board/parliament
    • Citizens' groups
    • Media

3. Coordination
    • Separate
    • Integrated

4. Monitoring
    • Reporting requirement on WID
    • WID action on project-reporting format
    • Statistical reporting on WID budget

5. Evaluation
    • Guidelines
    • Checklists
    • WID/gender issues in TOR
    • WID/gender specialists in missions

6. Personnel Policy
    • Quotas
    • Targets
    • Career development policies

administrative structures of responsibility for women. By the end of the Decade for Women all four donor agencies as well as the two national governments had set up their WID responsibility structures.

The structure and function of these offices with a responsibility for WID have been subject to heated debate. Agencies and governments have experimented with different structures and functions, and these periodic shifts have often created confusion and insecurity in WID offices. Though many of these WID offices have been in existence for nearly two decades, it appears that neither the donor agencies nor the national governments have yet made up their mind where these offices fit in the overall organizational structure, and what their main mission is. The donors have followed a common pattern. They started with single WID advisory positions in the late 1970s, increased WID resources in the mid 1980s and created separate WID divisions, but by 1992–93 the agencies had moved away from separate WID divisions to either single advisory positions or to the so-called flat structure in which the programme team is coequal with several other teams working on cross-cutting themes. The national governments in Tanzania and Bangladesh followed a similar pattern, starting first with WID advisory positions in the president/prime minister's office, and later moving on to create separate ministries or separate departments within ministries. Even after almost twenty years, these special machineries in donor agencies and national governments have remained largely peripheral to the mainstream of the agencies' and governments' work.

Donor agencies

The agencies have debated several issues regarding the location and function of WID/GAD responsibility structures: Should there be separate administrative units with their own staff and budget, or should there be only advisory positions? Should WID/GAD offices be closer to policy or closer to operations? Should these offices have only advocacy, policymaking and monitoring functions or should they also have a management and implementation role? Do these offices facilitate mainstreaming or hinder it?

Structure

In the last two decades donors have often shifted their positions on the debated issues. Initially all four donors created single WID advisory positions in central locations in the organizations. CIDA appointed a WID coordinator in 1976 in the policy branch; NORAD a WID consultant in 1979 in the country programme department; the World Bank its first WID advisor in 1975 in the vice-president's office; and the UNDP a WID advisor in 1976 in the bureau of policy planning and evaluation. These advisory positions were all at junior levels and lacked a voice in the agencies' decisionmaking bodies.

After nearly a decade of working with single advisory positions, donors came forward with enhanced resources and status for WID. The 1985 Nairobi Conference created the momentum for separate WID administrative units to be created with staff and budget in three of the four agencies. CIDA established its WID directorate in 1983, and the UNDP and the World Bank created their WID divisions in 1986 and 1987 respectively. NORAD decided against establishing a separate WID unit, arguing that it would work against mainstreaming, but it increased WID resources by creating two WID advisory positions. Thus, all the donors allocated regular budget staff and consultancy resources for WID. In several agencies, in addition to separate WID units, WID coordinators were appointed in geographical departments and WID specialists were placed in resident missions. In many field offices, nationals of partner countries were recruited as WID focal points.

The heads of the WID administrative units in CIDA and UNDP were given senior management status and participated in corporate decisionmaking bodies, but at the World Bank the position of WID director was established at junior management level – four levels below the top management – and she did not have a direct voice in decision-making. At NORAD, too, the senior WID advisor did not have senior management status, though she did participate in meetings of the project approval board. However, as part of a reorganization effort both the UNDP and the World Bank abolished their separate WID divisions, in 1992 and 1993 respectively, and created GAD programmes. CIDA, too, abolished the WID directorate in 1993 and went back to having a single WID advisory position. The restructuring essentially lowered the status of the heads of these programmes in the corporate hierarchy. But in several instances staff resources for WID remained unchanged. At UNDP and the World Bank GAD programmes retained their regular budget and staff resources. At CIDA, the staff resources from the WID directorate moved to regional departments, as new WID coordinators' posts were created. At the World Bank, too, regional WID coordinators' posts in Africa and Asia were retained.

Functions

How have the WID responsibility structures functioned in the last two decades? How have the agencies mandated and resourced them? Generally, WID responsibility structures have been mandated with advocacy, coordination and monitoring roles, leaving responsibility for implementing WID policies in the hands of programme managers. But though WID responsibility was formally allocated to programme managers, many of these officers had neither the time nor the expertise to address gender issues, and in reality it was the WID offices which had to shoulder the main responsibility for providing technical support to operational managers. The catalytic and promotional role of WID thus involved a heavy workload, including the development of policy and strategy as well as technical support to operational departments. In trying to perform both functions WID offices were often stretched too thin. As a result long-term policy and strategy-development suffered. For example, a recent evaluation of CIDA's WID policy found that 'the heavy workload of the Directorate staff, day to day, as primary resource officers and secondary resource officers had tended to "crowd out" the important but seldom urgent functions of research, policy and strategy development. There are too few staff in the WID Directorate to fulfill both functions effectively, even too few to fulfill one completely adequately.'[1]

Resources

Inadequacy of resources has frequently been cited as a major constraint by the WID offices. WID offices were generally given two to four regular budget professional positions (in the general headquarters NORAD had two, UNDP three, CIDA four), buttressed by consultancies and extra budgetary resources. For example, CIDA had nearly twenty WID consultants in the headquarters, who often performed staff functions. In 1992, the WID division of the World Bank had six full-time consultants and almost an equal number of regular budget staff. In addition it had WID coordinators in three regional departments – Asia, Africa and EMNA.[2]

Though the WID programmes often complained that other comparable programmes such as environment and population received greater agency resources, the higher management of the agencies argued that the WID resources were at a similar level, and that instead of being too ambitious, WID offices should do less, be selective, and more strategic.[3] Dependence on consultants also received mixed reviews in agencies. Although consultants offered technical expertise and flexibility, they lacked the authority, access, and continuity in the organization which only regular budget staff could provide. CIDA evaluation found, for example, that consultants were used so extensively that a 'parallel delivery system for WID developed'.[4] In the multilateral agencies, consultants were generally dependent on extra budgetary resources from a few donor agencies, which placed them in an even more vulnerable position in the organization.

Staffing patterns

WID positions, especially in field offices, were created at a junior level, which was often a constraint on influencing operational programmes. In resident missions or field offices, WID positions were generally staffed by either junior agency officials or by locally recruited expatriate consultants or nationals – in other words, people who lacked status and authority in the corporate hierarchy. In many cases WID specialists were assigned responsibilities outside the official bilateral country programme framework, coordinating WID, and NGO work. This structural placement outside the country programme framework weakened WID specialists' capacity to influence policy dialogues or country programming exercises. Important documents were not routed through WID specialists as a matter of routine, and in many instances they were asked to comment on documents or brief consultants at the last moment as an afterthought.[5] In some agencies, like NORAD, WID focal point responsibilities in headquarters were assigned to staff in different departments in addition to their regular jobs and without clearly assigned staff time. Lacking time and expertise, these staff could do very little to address gender issues in their daily work routine.

Staffing for WID positions remained a problem. In most agencies (an exception being the World Bank), WID units were staffed entirely by women, and other WID positions in the headquarters and in the field were also staffed by women. The image of WID positions being 'women's jobs' made them appear less professional. In the agencies, men and even women interested in furthering their career path were reluctant to serve in these positions, as there was no incentive or reward attached to them, and performing well in these positions did not facilitate career advancement on the corporate ladder. Indeed, WID positions were often regarded as dead-end jobs.[6] Many ambitious women within agencies avoided these positions for fear of being typecast as 'WID'. The negative image of WID positions – as less professional jobs which any woman can do – was further exacerbated by the recruitment of wives of embassy or agency personnel for these positions in the field offices. While a spouse employment policy was in general a positive step, the concentration of wives in WID jobs undermined the posts' image of expertise and professionalism, as this type of staffing decision appeared to many outsiders to be based on nepotism and patronage.

Did the creation of WID administrative units and offices facilitate or hinder the mainstreaming of WID/GAD responsibilities? It appears that structures made very little difference. WID offices in NORAD as well as in CIDA equally pushed to foreground gender issues, though the latter created a separate WID directorate and the former did not. The critical factors appear to be not structure, but the definition of mission, resources, commitment and accountability measures to ensure agency compliance. In all the agencies, WID offices were given a catalytic role – they raised issues and provided ideas – but the responsibility of implementation was in the hands of programme managers and mission heads. Agencies gave programme managers WID responsibility, but they did not devise or enforce measures to hold managers accountable for WID. In the absence of institutionalized accountability the performance of managers varied greatly. To a large extent it depended on their personal commitment and that of WID staff.

Development partners

In Bangladesh and Tanzania, semi-official national women's organizations and separate women's wings in political parties and trade unions existed even before the Decade for Women. However, offices within the government responsible for women were set up only during the Decade. It cannot be argued that there was a strong domestic pressure to create women's machineries in either of these two countries: the impetus came mostly from outside. As many international organizations and national governments started to set up special machineries, Bangladesh and Tanzania followed their examples.

Structures

In Bangladesh, the government established offices responsible for women for the first time in 1976. The decision came as a surprise, since the women's organizations had not demanded the establishment of WID offices. It appears that the military government of Ziaur Rahman, which assumed power as a result of a coup d'état in 1975, wanted to project a modernist, development-oriented image and found WID to be a good vehicle for that purpose. The regime also wanted to increase the volume of donor assistance, and therefore picked up on some of the donors' favourite themes: population and women. An additional incentive was the recruitment of political support among new groups, and women were identified as a potentially large constituency.

The government set up a national women's organization – Bangladesh Jatiya Mahila Sangstha (BJMS) – in February 1976, which was given wide-ranging functions. In April 1976, a special assistant to the president for women's affairs was appointed, primarily with an advocacy and advisory role. In December 1976, a Women's Affairs Division was created, which gave the special assistant both staff and budget. In 1978, a full-fledged ministry with a separate minister for women's affairs was established, which was later combined with the social welfare ministry under a single minister for social welfare and women's affairs. In addition to the women's ministry and the BJMS, the planning commission also had a focal point for women but it was located at a relatively junior level. The government has also recently assigned WID focal point responsibilities to staff in ministries from different sectors.

In Tanzania, too, initially the office responsible for women was placed strategically in a central location, with a minister without portfolio in the prime minister's office. In 1984, she received staff and a budget as part of Tanzania's preparation for the 1985 UN Women's Conference. The national machinery, however, was later moved away from the prime minister's office and became part of the Ministry of Local Government, Community Development and Cooperatives. In recent years Tanzania has also initiated a system of WID focal points in different sectoral ministries and in the planning commission.

Functions

The structure and function of the national machineries has followed the same pattern as that of WID offices in donor agencies, moving from single advisory positions in strategic central locations, primarily with an advocacy function, to a separate sectoral ministry heavily involved in the implementation of field projects. The problems faced by national machineries – lack of status, access, resources and staffing – have mirrored those of donor agencies.

The national machineries initially emphasized advocacy work. Many feminists in Bangladesh and Tanzania urged the national machineries to prioritize policy development and monitoring functions, and not get bogged down in the implementation of special women's projects. For example, following the first regional South and Southeast Asian WID Conference held in Bangladesh, a group of Bangladeshi women submitted a memorandum to the government in 1977 urging the national machinery to take a mainstreaming approach, and arguing that the national machinery's main roles should be strategy development, monitoring, and coordination. The capacities of sectoral ministries and other important government offices, such as the Planning Commission and Bureau of Statistics, should be strengthened to address gender issues in their work. To ensure institutional ownership, the memorandum suggested that the sectoral ministries should establish their own taskforces comprising both women and men to suggest ways and means of addressing gender issues in their policies and programmes.[8] The line of argument in the Bangladesh memorandum was very similar to that which CIDA and NORAD adopted a few years later in their WID policies. The government of Bangladesh, however, ignored the feminists' plea for a mainstreaming approach. The women's movement was relatively weak and could not mobilize public support to lobby for their vision of the national machinery. A year after the memorandum, the government created a separate women's ministry which started to prioritize the implementation of special training and income-generating projects for women. The ready availability of donor assistance for such field projects worked as an incentive. Strengthening the institutional capacity of the national machineries for policy work and for monitoring has become an item on the donors' agenda only in the last few years.

In Tanzania the national machinery did develop a national policy on women; it also worked on legal reforms. But here too the machinery got increasingly involved in implementation of special women's projects at the donors' behest, and only recently have donors turned their attention to building the capacity of the national machinery.

Staffing of national machineries was yet another problem in the partner countries, as there were very few senior women in the government services. In Bangladesh, for example, not a single career service senior female administrator was available to head the women's department and directorate. Male officials were reluctant to serve, which meant that the ministry became primarily a dumping-ground for male officials who were about to retire or found themselves in official disfavour, and there was a quick turnover of officials. In Tanzania, too, many posts in the Women's Ministry were left vacant. The national machineries in both countries remained institutionally weak.

ACCOUNTABILITY

The donor agencies and national governments have generally been more preoccupied with WID responsibility structures than with elaborating or enforcing accountability for WID mandates. Only CIDA's 1984 WID policy highlighted the importance of accountability in managing systemic change. One of CIDA's objectives was to 'operationalize WID policy in a manner that is measurable and reviewable and that includes both accountability systems and support mechanisms'.[9] The other donors and governments did not specify their WID accountability measures, though donors have increasingly turned their attention to accountability as a key to ensuring organizational compliance with WID mandates.

Internal accountability

Donor agencies have experimented with several instruments to ensure internal accountability for WID, such as staff performance appraisal, project/programme screening, approval, evaluation and so on. The two national governments have not yet attempted to introduce any internal accountability measures.

CIDA and to a limited extent UNDP have used annual staff performance appraisal to hold staff accountable for WID. CIDA's 1986 WID Action Plan gave all branches responsibility to: (a) ask employees to specify WID responsibility where applicable in their work-plan objectives; and (b) take performance on WID into account in staff performance appraisal. CIDA's rationale was that 'officers will allocate time and resources to WID only if they have responsibility to do so, have necessary resources and are required by performance appraisals and job descriptions to meet specific performance criteria'.[10] The CIDA WID assessment, however, found that performance review did not work very well. It was 'too vague and diffuse, when everyone is responsible, no one is responsible'.[11] The assessment argued that, rather than making all agency staff accountable, it would be more effective to hold only key managers (operations managers, vice-presidents and country programme directors) accountable for WID achievements.

UNDP's experiences with performance appraisal were more recent and limited. It was introduced on an experimental basis in the Bureau of Policy, Planning, and Evaluation in the hope that it would introduce a 'rewards system' and motivate middle-management staff, interested in moving up the corporate ladder, to improve their WID performance.[12] Its effectiveness is yet to be assessed.

At NORAD it was argued that since the agency did not have a hierarchical corporate management style, introducing WID as an item of performance appraisal would not be an effective way of holding agency staff accountable for WID.[13] The World Bank and the two national governments did have a top-down administrative structure, but they did not try to use WID criteria in staff performance appraisal.

Project/programme screening was another instrument used by donor agencies to ensure WID compliance. WID advisors and offices in NORAD, CIDA and UNDP participated in project approval boards, which could be used as checkpoints to hold operational programmes in line with WID goals. CIDA's WID office appears to have exercised a strong authority in project approval decisions. CIDA's WID evaluation noted that many existing projects in CIDA were 'WID retrofitted'.[14] The World Bank did not introduce any project screening procedure, nor did the WID office have any voice in project/programme approval.

In the two national governments the ministers in charge of women's affairs did participate in cabinet meetings, the highest decisionmaking body, but there is no evidence that apart from promoting the policies and programmes of their own ministries they used the opportunity to hold other sectoral ministries accountable for WID goals. Consideration of WID/GAD criteria in corporate and programme and project evaluations was yet another means of ensuring WID accountability. But, as will be discussed later, no donor agency systematically used WID/GAD criteria in evaluations.

Accountability was difficult to introduce and enforce for a variety of reasons. The goals of WID policies were usually not stated in measurable terms and no target or time table set, so it was difficult to review and measure the WID performance of agency staff for non-specific WID 'integration'. In the absence of institutionalized targets, enforcement of accountability depended to a large extent on the personal commitment and monitoring of top decisionmakers. Here agency experiences varied and commitment at the top varied with changes in corporate heads. CIDA's WID evaluation, for instance, found that despite a conscious emphasis on accountability, WID strategies and Project Approval Memorandum (PAM)/WID annexes provided only 'a partial framework' for WID monitoring and evaluation, that the memorandum of understanding with development partners lacked 'enforceable WID conditions'; and that 'the inclusion of WID in officers' performance appraisals and in project and programme evaluations have tended to become "mechanical" or "neglected".'[15]

Public accountability

Public accountability was stronger in the two bilateral agencies than the two multilateral ones, because the former worked under greater public scrutiny. Both NORAD and CIDA reported through their ministries to parliament, whose debates were held in the public domain. Being ultimately responsible to their taxpaying citizens, NORAD and CIDA had to be accountable to public interest groups. The NGOs, feminist lobby groups, and media, which were highly vocal on women's issues in Norway and Canada, worked as watchdogs on the two agencies.

In contrast, the work of the two multilateral agencies – UNDP and the World Bank – was largely shielded from the scrutiny of public interest groups. These multilateral agencies reported directly to their governing boards, which consisted of representatives of different governments. The discussions of the governing boards generally took place outside the glare of public attention. Media and citizens' groups had very little access to these discussions, or to the documents prepared by the multilateral organizations. The World Bank's documents were the most restricted. In the absence of information and access, it was difficult for women's lobbies and public interest groups to act as watchdogs on the UNDP and the World Bank. Only recently have some public interest groups been successful in bringing pressure on the Bank's operations – for example, the Bank's lending for the Narmada Dam project in India was cancelled as a result of lobbying by the environmentalists. Women's organizations, however, have not been able to exert a similar pressure on the Bank's specific operations.

Public accountability was weak in the two partner countries. The institutions that ensured public accountability in the donor countries – multiparty system, parliament, media and citizens' groups – did not function in the same way in the partner countries. In Tanzania, the ruling party dominated the government and parliament. In Bangladesh, opposition political parties were active inside and outside parliament but few political parties seriously championed gender equality. Ten per cent of parliamentary seats in Bangladesh were reserved for women, but even those women who came to parliament under the women's quota rarely took the initiative to ask tough questions and hold their government accountable for their actions on women's advancement. This failure is understandable, because the women parliamentarians were elected neither by a female constituency nor by a general constituency, but were primarily composed of party loyalists, selected by members of the majority party in parliament. They never campaigned on gender issues.

The media, NGOs and citizens' groups also did not enjoy the same freedom in Tanzania and Bangladesh as they did in the donor countries. In Bangladesh and Tanzania the number of NGOs and women's organizations have multiplied in the last two decades, due largely to donor funding. But many of these organizations, especially the NGOs, emphasized a delivery-of-services approach rather than advocacy and lobbying for policy change, and were heavily involved in implementing development projects funded by the donors. Since donor funding in most cases had to be channelled through the governments, the NGOs avoided the path of open criticism of government actions. Unlike the NGOs and women's organizations of the donor countries, who were able freely to scrutinize and debate their governments' policies and demand changes, the NGOs and women's organizations in the partner countries had to tread a fine line between their autonomous stance and being perceived as inimical to the state.

Establishing donors' accountability to their development partners is another major challenge that is yet to be addressed by the agencies. Generally, donors believe that partner countries should be made accountable, since they are on the receiving end of funds, but rarely do the donors feel accountable to the partners – though many of their policy prescriptions often lead to disastrous results for the partners. Additionally, aid is generally negotiated between governments. Citizens' groups, particularly women's groups, have no participation in the aid negotiations and they are generally left uninformed about the donors' policy packages and their potential impact on the people. Yet in the final analysis it is the citizens – women and men – of the partner countries who live with the consequences of assistance and repay the debt. Establishing reciprocal accountability between donors and aid recipients, especially accountability to the citizens of partner countries, remains a priority task for the future.

COORDINATION

In the last two decades neither the donors nor their partners have been able to come forward with satisfactory coordination mechanisms. Only the two bilateral donors established separate WID coordinating bodies; the two multilateral agencies had no formal coordination mechanism. In Tanzania and Bangladesh national women's coordination councils were established, but they existed largely on paper.

Norway established a separate WID advisory/coordination committee, the Arbeidsutralget for Kvinnerettet Bistand (AUK), which met regularly for only a few years, before running into a number of problems. There was a high turnover of members; too many issues were brought to AUK, and too late;[16] the reorganization of governmental agencies, which made NORAD more autonomous, also made AUK's work difficult. Since 1989 informal contacts and discussions have replaced the formal meetings of AUK.

In contrast, the WID coordinating body of CIDA, the WID Steering Committee, met regularly. Established in 1977, it was relatively large and included representation from agency-wide management-level staff. The Committee was composed of roughly thirty senior branch managers – usually the deputy directors – and the WID directorate staff. It met once every three months, and was mandated to advise the president's committee in matters relating to the implementation of CIDA's WID Policy and Plan of Action, monitored the results, and prepared an annual report. CIDA's WID policy evaluation found that the Steering Committee provided a good forum for the exchange of information and identification of problems, but it did not have enough authority to ensure agency-wide compliance.[17]

Coordination was most problematic in the partner countries. In both

Tanzania and Bangladesh, governments established national women's coordination councils but these bodies rarely met. NGOs and autonomous women's organizations were reluctant to be 'coordinated' by the national machineries, as they feared that this might result in their control over them. On the other hand, coordination among the NGOs and autonomous women's organizations was also difficult, though at periodic intervals they did form common-cause coalitions around single issues. Thus in Bangladesh in 1987 major women's organizations formed a common coalition, Oikkya Baddha Nari Samaj (the United Women's Front), to rally public support to stop violence against women. In 1993 again NGOs and autonomous women's organizations started coordinating amongst themselves for the preparations of the World Conference on Women (WCW '95). Over one hundred organizations came together to form a national committee for the preparation of WCW '95.

Coordination between donors in aid-recipient countries was another thorny issue. In both Tanzania and Bangladesh a large number of donors funded WID projects and programmes. In Bangladesh, donors established their own coordination mechanism, Local Consultative Group (LCG), which was convened by the World Bank. The Bangladesh government was invited to participate in LCG meetings, and the donors' WID network was active and gained status as a subcommittee of the LCG. During the formulation of Bangladesh's fourth five-year plan, the WID network actively facilitated the inclusion of gender issues in the plan, as well as in donors' policy dialogues. WID was placed as an agenda item in the LCG meeting for the first time in 1989, and was later raised in the annual aid consortium meeting in Paris. A joint government–donor WID taskforce was created in 1990, which established five working groups to review existing projects and programmes in different sectors and come forward with major recommendations.

In Tanzania, by contrast, the donors' WID network was relatively inactive. WID never featured as an agenda item in the donors' consultative meetings, which were convened by the UNDP. Nor was there any joint government–donor task force. A joint donor–government–NGOs WID network was briefly active in the 1980s but later became moribund, as the overburdened national machinery could not organize regular meetings. A few donors, such as the Netherlands, have again started to take an interest in creating a forum for coordination, but donors have by and large felt that the initiative should come from the government. Some donors have argued that the government deliberately did not attempt to coordinate donors' efforts, as it wanted to improve its bargaining position in project negotiations with different donors.[18]

MONITORING

All the donors introduced some monitoring mechanisms to assess the implementation of their WID/GAD mandates and policies. Generally, three types of monitoring device were used: annual reporting require-ments; WID action on project-reporting formats; and statistical reporting on donor assistance. The annual reporting requirements were generally descriptive, and summed up the agency's WID activities: as such they had limited value in measuring progress towards WID policy objectives. The other two tools – WID action on project reporting formats and statistical reporting of donor assistance – could however be used as measures of 'integration' and 'mainstreaming'.

All the donors introduced annual reporting requirements. Since 1987, Norway's annual reports to parliament on development assistance have included a separate chapter on WID. CIDA's WID Steering Committee prepared annual reports listing the WID initiatives of the agency. And after the creation of WID divisions, the annual reports of the World Bank as well as those of UNDP started to include a separate section on WID. Additionally, during 1989–90 UNDP undertook an agency-wide review of the implementation of its WID policy that was intended to create the database for future monitoring.[19]

The two bilateral donors introduced a mandatory WID classification system on projects. CIDA required all projects to include a PAM WID Annex which was monitored by CIDA's corporate memory. NORAD's statistical unit also monitored the agency's WID classification of projects. Both NORAD and CIDA adopted OECD/DAC's statistical reporting format on WID assistance which classified women-oriented aid into two categories: 'WID-specific' and 'WID-integrated'. 'WID-specific' assistance counted the full value of each project in which women were the sole target group as agents and beneficiaries. 'WID-integrated' assistance, on the other hand, covered the full value of each project in which women were identified explicitly as part of the target group as agents and/or beneficiaries of all main components of the project. To be counted, projects had to fulfil four DAC criteria: 'Women from the recipient countries ... with priority given to the target population (1) must be consulted in the design of the project ... (2) must be active participants during implementation of the project ... (3) barriers to female participation ... must be identified ... and measures designed ... to overcome the barriers and (4) WID expertise must be utilized throughout the project cycle.'[20]

The OECD/DAC's statistical classification had certain limitations. It could be used to classify projects which had an identified target popu-lation. But a large portion of assistance – such as policy-lending, commodity-aid and so on – lacked a predetermined target population. The classification was also based on the project officers' own interpretation of whether the fourfold criteria were met. This could result in under-reporting or over-reporting. But despite the limitations, the statistical reporting format was a useful monitoring tool. It provided corporate leadership with a measurable yardstick with which to monitor the agency's progress in committing resources to WID, and could also be used to monitor inter-sectoral and inter-departmental WID performance.

The two bilateral donors also complied with the other OECD/DAC reporting requirements, which worked as additional monitoring mechanisms. NORAD and CIDA reported on WID activities and WID assistance in their annual memorandums to OECD, and they also reported regularly on the implementation of DAC/WID guiding principles. Since the adoption of the WID Guiding Principles in 1983, OECD/DAC has surveyed its members four times to monitor their implementation.[21]

The two multilateral donors adopted neither a mandatory WID classification of projects nor a system of statistical reporting of WID assistance. At UNDP, after the creation of the WID division, a project review process was introduced which required all new projects and a sample of ongoing projects to provide information on women's participation. UNDP conceptualized women's participation in a less rigorous manner than the bilateral donors; and unlike the bilateral agencies, who monitored WID classification of projects centrally, at UNDP the monitoring was left to the WID division. This was irregular and was discontinued after 1989. The staff at WID division argued that the instrument was of little use, as it was too mechanical and depended on the project officers' subjective interpretation.[22]

Like that of UNDP, the WID division at the World Bank started its own separate monitoring of WID 'intentions' in the Bank's projects. This was done by reviewing all staff appraisal reports (SARs) and classifying them into three categories by their treatment of WID issues: (1) operations with WID-specific actions; (2) operations with discussion of WID issues but no actions; and (3) no or superficial WID treatment. The monitoring reports on WID actions in SARs, classified by geographical regions and sectors, were regularly circulated by the WID division throughout the Bank and reported in the Bank's annual reports. The Bank's 1994 WID policy paper pledged to strengthen its monitoring system to assess the progress of gender analysis in economic and sector work and the linkages to Bank's lending operations.[23]

In the partner countries, the national machineries reported on their activities. For example, in Bangladesh the annual economic surveys prepared by the Ministry of Finance for budget submission included detailed reports by the Ministry of Women's Affairs of its activities and budget. But the countries are yet to adopt any system of mandatory WID classification of projects or statistical reporting of 'WID-integrated' budget.

As the donors have begun to assess their WID experiences, the inadequacy of monitoring mechanisms has emerged as a key issue. There is a growing recognition that up to now WID monitoring has been mainly 'process- and activity-oriented': it has emphasized WID 'intentions' and 'efforts' rather than 'results'. Agencies have generally monitored the adoption of instruments and procedures but not how these WID measures have influenced agency operations and affected aid recipients. A part of the problem has been the agencies' failure to establish key indicators to assess the achievement of their WID policy goals. The absence of targets within set time-periods was another constraint in monitoring WID achievements.

EVALUATION

Donors adopted several measures to include gender considerations in their evaluations, developing guidelines, checklists and specific methodologies which were included in their evaluation manuals. Agencies were required to include gender issues in the terms of reference (TOR) of evaluations and include women in evaluation teams.

Generally, bilateral donors made greater efforts to address gender issues in their evaluations. Norway prepared a WID checklist for evaluations, surveyed past evaluations to assess their consideration of gender issues, mandated inclusion of gender issues in the TORs of all evaluations concerned with social impact, and carried out field assessments of selected WID-integrated projects to draw lessons from successes and failures.[24] Norway also reviewed some of its WID instruments, such as its WID grant.[25] Similarly CIDA developed WID methodologies for evaluation at programme and project levels; it also carried out an assessment of its WID policy.[26] The UNDP's 1987 WID policy framework required the agency to integrate gender issues in its project evaluation procedures. The World Bank has also recently started to take an interest in developing the corporate mandate to address gender issues systematically in the evaluation of Bank-sponsored projects. The 1994 policy paper promised to carry out evaluation of implementation efforts on the ground.[27] The governments of Tanzania and Bangladesh are yet to come forward with WID/GAD guidelines for evaluation.

Despite corporate mandates, guidelines and methodologies, up to now only a small percentage of evaluations have addressed gender issues systematically. For example, a recent assessment of DAC donors found that, notwithstanding terms of reference, addressing gender issues in 70 per cent of a sample of agency operations, only about 40 per cent of evaluation reports contained a full discussion of gender issues.[28] Similarly a desk review of fifty general UNDP evaluations conducted in 1987 found marginal treatment of WID/GAD issues.[29] Many of the available agency evaluations are on women-specific programmes and projects; only a small number of policy evaluations have addressed gender issues.

Lack of field-based data is a major problem for WID assessment. Most of the project and programme interventions do not collect baseline data; hence it is difficult to measure progress towards gender equality or women's advancement. The majority of assessments of WID policies and measures are based on donor agency staff's impressions of effectiveness and progress rather than field-based hard data.

PERSONNEL POLICY

The donor agencies as well as their partner countries adopted several policy instruments to increase the number of women on their staff: quotas, targets and career development policies were the three most frequently used. The two multilateral donors did not formally adopt any of these three instruments, though their corporate leadership publicly expressed a concern to increase women's numbers in their agencies, particularly in management positions. The two bilateral donors, by contrast, adopted either a system of quota (NORAD) or targets (CIDA). They also took on gender-responsive career development policies to retain female staff. Tanzania and Bangladesh also used a female quota system in recruitment.

Bilateral donors

Norway's WID strategy of 1985 recommended that female applicants who fulfilled the selection requirements be given precedence for initial and further occupational training and for employment and promotion in categories where women are in a minority. Between 1985 and 1992 NORAD succeeded in increasing women's representation from 28 to 43 per cent among senior professionals and from 7 to 16 per cent among senior management. NORAD also adopted gender-sensitive career development policies, such as spouse employment and leave policies, to motivate women to go on overseas assignments.

Instead of a quota system, CIDA used the more dynamic system of 'targeting' to achieve employment equity over a certain period of time. Following the government's employment equity policy, which called on all government agencies to analyse the representation of women and develop action plans which set targets to attain employment equity, CIDA established its first action plan for equal opportunities for women in 1975. The agency monitored the implementation of targets, reporting achievements as well as shortfalls. Between 1977 and 1991, through its employment equity policy, CIDA increased the percentage of women in management categories from zero to 17 per cent and in administrative and foreign service categories from 20 to 45 per cent.

Multilateral donors

Unlike the two bilateral donors, UNDP made no effort to establish and monitor targets for the recruitment and promotion of women. Predictably, women's share of employment in professional and management categories increased much more slowly. In the eighteen years between 1975 and 1993 women's representation in professional categories increased from 20 to 26 per cent; the increase in senior management categories was from 3 to 8 per cent only.

In its 1990 report to the governing council reviewing the progress of implementation of its WID policy, UNDP for the first time addressed the issue of personnel policy and discussed its various dimensions: women's share of employment, recruitment of consultants and project staff, and career development of female staff. It reported that though 50 per cent of entry-level career-track professionals joining UNDP during 1988–89 through its management training programme were women, only 6 per cent of resident representatives and 17 per cent of deputy resident representatives were women. The report described the special measures UNDP was undertaking to recruit more women, particularly in management and senior positions. The report, however, underscored the problem of retention of women staff and stressed the need to institute a wide range of 'gender-sensitive conditions of service and entitlement' for women's career development – such as assistance with spouse employment in the field, flexitime for staff with childcare or elder-care responsibilities, flexible maternity-leave provision, concurrent reassignment of career couples to serve in the same duty station, and training of senior management on gender issues in the workplace. The official policies regarding service and entitlement have not yet been modified, but at least the need for creating gender-sensitive employment and working conditions has been formally articulated.

Of all the agencies studied, women's share of employment is the lowest in the World Bank. In professional and managerial categories it rose from 1 to 17 per cent in eighteen years (1976–93), though when all job categories are included women constitute 28 per cent of the Bank's employees. A report produced in 1989 by the Status of Women Working Group of the staff association identified several factors that contributed to women's marginalization in the Bank – a non-supportive working environment, the 'old boys' network', and misperception of women as being either too aggressive or not aggressive enough for management positions.[30] A more recent report by the Advisory Group on Higher Level Women in the Bank noted several additional constraints – gender biases during interview, lack of supportive policies for dual-career households, lack of career development opportunities, double standards for behaviour, gender-based discrimination and sexual harassment. The report recommended a three-pronged strategy: increasing external recruitment, enlarging the pipeline of women candidates for senior and management positions through improved career development, and building a productive work environment free of discrimination.[31]

Partner countries

Instead of setting targets to achieve employment equity, the governments of Tanzania and Bangladesh adopted a female-quota system in public-sector recruitment. But the female quota in entry-level jobs only ensured women's presence in lower positions; the senior management jobs remained virtually unaffected. For example, Bangladesh adopted a 10 per cent female quota for public service jobs in 1976, which was later increased to 15 per cent. After a decade women constituted 11 per cent of public-sector employees, but only 0.02 per cent of senior decisionmaking jobs were held by women.[32] In Tanzania, too, only 3 per cent of managers and 4 per cent of top administrative decisionmakers were women.[33]

Women's groups advocated the adoption of several affirmative-action instruments, such as lateral entry of qualified women from other services into senior administrative/management-level jobs on contract, preparation of a roster of qualified women candidates for senior-level positions, and so on. But the governments were not forthcoming in considering these suggestions. For example, though the Bangladesh government had encouraged the lateral entry of army officials into senior civil-service jobs on contract, it had not pursued a similar policy to encourage the entry of women officials from education, health and social welfare into these positions.

SUMMARY

Beginning with a tenuous foothold in the late 1970s, WID/GAD has by the 1990s become a legitimate institutional concern both in the donor agencies and in their partner governments. The establishment of WID responsibility structures was often the first and major step in WID institutionalization, and although the structure and function of these offices varied there appears to be a common pattern. Starting with single WID advisory positions, agencies and governments increased WID resources in the mid 1980s, but by the early 1990s WID-specific resources shrank, though WID/GAD remained a priority theme of assistance.

Donors and their partners adopted a variety of measures which succeeded in institutionalizing WID in agency processes and procedures, but there remained a gap between formal institutionalization and actual practice. For example, coordination mechanisms were mostly left unused. Accountability measures were difficult to enforce because agencies and governments rarely established goals measurable over a time period against which they could be held accountable. Monitoring measures were weak. Only the two bilateral donors adopted mandatory WID classification of projects and budgets which attempted to measure the agency's commitment to resourcing WID. Again, it is the two bilateral donors who actively pursued affirmative action personnel policies through quotas and targets. The multilateral donors, in contrast, did not adopt employment equity policies, which partially explains women's smaller numbers among their staff.

There was also a gap between the donors and their partners. Most of the WID instruments were designed by the donors, and the partner governments often borrowed these donor-designed instruments without first assessing their use and effectiveness in the specific national contexts.

NOTES

1. CIDA, *Gender as a Cross Cutting Theme in Development Assistance – An Evaluation of CIDA's WID Policy and Activities, 1984–1992*, Executive Summary, July 1993, p. 11.

2. The number of staff and consultants varied a great deal in the donor agencies from year to year.

3. Personal interviews, NORAD and UNDP, 1991.

4. CIDA, *Gender as a Cross Cutting Theme*, p. 10.

5. Personal interviews, NORAD, CIDA and UNDP, 1991.

6. Case study, commissioned by OECD/DAC, *Assessment of Policies and*

Organizational Measures in WID Adopted by DAC Member Donor Organizations, mimeo, 1993.

7. CIDA, *Gender as a Cross-Cutting Theme.*

8. Rounaq Jahan and Hanna Papanek, eds., *Women and Development: Perspectives from South and South East Asia,* Bangladesh Institute of Law and International Affairs, Dhaka 1979, pp. 18–20.

9. CIDA, *Women in Development Policy Framework,* 1984, p. 4.

10. Elizabeth McAllister, *Managing the Process of Change: Women in Development,* CIDA 1989, p. 3.

11. CIDA, *Gender as a Cross Cutting Theme,* p. 12.

12. Personal interviews, UNDP, 1991.

13. Personal interviews, NORAD, 1991.

14. CIDA, *Gender as a Cross Cutting Theme,* p. 3.

15. Ibid., p. 12.

16. Personal interviews, NORAD, 1991.

17. CIDA, *CIDA's Women in Development Programme: Evaluation Assessment Report,* December 1990.

18. Personal interviews with donor agencies, Dar-es-Salaam, 1992.

19. UNDP, *Women in Development: Report of the Administrator 1990.*

20. OECD/DAC, *Methodology for Statistical Reporting of Women-Oriented Aid Activities,* 1989, pp. 3–4.

21. OECD/DAC, *The Third Monitoring Report on the Implementation of the DAC Revised Guiding Principles on WID,* Paris 1990; USAID and DDA, *Assessment of Policies and Organizational Measures in Women in Development Adopted by DAC Member Countries,* mimeo, 1994.

22. Personal interviews, UNDP, 1991.

23. The World Bank, *Enhancing Women's Participation in Economic Development,* 1994, p. 69.

24. The Royal Norwegian Ministry of Development Cooperation, *Norway's Strategy for Assistance to Women in Development,* 1985.

25. Janne Lexow and Desmond McNeill, *The Women's Grant,* Evaluation Report, NORAD, Oslo 1989.

26. CIDA, *Gender As a Cross Cutting Theme.*

27. The World Bank, *Enhancing Women's Participation in Economic Development.*

28. Zulia Z. Paton, *WID as a Cross-Cutting Issue in Development Aid Evaluations,* CIDA, 1994.

29. UNDP, 'Women in UNDP-Supported Projects: A Review of How UNDP Project Evaluations Deal with Gender Issues', New York, May 1987.

30. The World Bank Staff Association, *Report on Status of Higher Level Women in the World Bank Group,* November 1989.

31. The World Bank, *Excellence through Equality: An Increased Role for Women in the World Bank: A Report of the Advisory Group on Higher Level Women's Issues,* April 1992, p. 2.

32. Women for Women, *Women and National Planning in Bangladesh,* Dhaka 1990, p. 2.

33. NORAD, *Action Plan for WID Tanzania,* mimeo, p. 12.

CHAPTER 4

OPERATIONAL STRATEGIES

Here's a situation. There is a 55 year old Director of a Country Operations Department. He's an economist – he could be from any country. He deals with heads of state and ministers, and he insists on quantitative economic evidence. If you talk to him about any specific measure to help women, such as in agriculture, he'll ask where is your information on cost effectiveness or how much this intervention will improve productivity.

Barbara Herz, quoted in A. Rao et al., *Gender Training and Development Planning: Learning from Experience*, Population Council, 1992, p. 20

Along with institutionalization, WID operationalization was a major concern of donor agencies and their development partners. Over the years, means used to influence agency operations included guidelines, training, research, special projects, analytical tools, country programming, macro-policies, and policy dialogue (see Figure 4.1). A few donors, such as CIDA and NORAD, adopted a coherent set of strategies to influence operations as part of their WID action plans, while others developed instruments and procedures gradually. Again, it is difficult to assess the actual use of these tools and their influence on operations, since they were not systematically monitored by agencies.

GUIDELINES

This was one of the earliest strategies used by the donors. All four donors developed detailed guidance for their operations; by contrast, the partner governments did not adopt similar guidelines. Some donors, such as UNDP, classified their guidelines under 'special considerations'; others, like CIDA, integrated the guidelines in the programme and project cycle. Both general and sectoral guidelines were used. Some donors, such as NORAD, established targets and timetables; others used only broad programming directions.

NORAD

NORAD's 1985 WID strategy and action plan laid down long-term guidelines and short-term action plans for the coming year aimed at the various sectors and channels of development assistance.[1] Two common

Figure 4.1 Operational Strategies

1. Guidelines
   - Project
   - Sector
   - Country programme

2. Training
   - Separate
   - Integrated
   - Awareness and sensitivity
   - Skill and expertise

3. Research
   - Gender-disaggregated statistics and data
   - Operational research
   - Policy analysis
   - Theoretical research

4. Special Projects
   - Innovation
   - Empowerment
   - Upscaling
   - Mainstreaming

5. Analytical Tools
   - Gender analysis
   - Consultation with target population

6. Country Programming
   - WID/gender country profile and strategy
   - Gender issues in country assistance strategy
   - WID components in major sectors/programmes
   - Five-year/annual development plans

7. Macro-policies
   - Gendered analysis
   - Gendered action

8. Policy Dialogue
   - Gendered participation
   - Gendered agenda

actions recommended for implementation during 1985–86 were: a review of existing assistance to evaluate its impact on women, and preparation of a plan to make assistance 'women-oriented'. The guidelines set a few quantitative targets. For example, they stipulated that by the year 1990, in the priority agricultural sector, 20 per cent of all assistance should benefit women; in fellowship assistance the proportion of women should be increased to 50 per cent by the year 1991; in technical assistance at least 30 per cent of women's participation should be ensured in feasibility studies, project reviews and evaluations; and in job categories where women constituted less than 30 per cent of the workforce, qualified women applicants should be given precedence.

Though NORAD's guidelines and actions were largely integrationist by nature, geared to help women catch up with men, in several instances women's alternative vision and priorities and their special needs were also given a significant weight. For example, women's traditional knowledge and skills in different sectors were identified as areas of long- and short-term assistance. Similarly, women's special needs related to maternity benefits and childcare were also recognized.

Internal assessments reveal that only a limited number of the guidelines and short-term actions were actually implemented. The numerical targets established in the agricultural sector and in personnel were achieved, but the recommendations regarding the review and preparation of sector plans were largely ignored. Within NORAD, opinion varied with regard to the efficacy of WID sector plans. Those in favour argued that WID sector guidelines would facilitate the task of project officers and experts, who generally have limited expertise about how to address gender issues in the sectoral programmes and projects. Opponents felt that national and cultural differences often make standardized guidelines meaningless, and that projects should be based on the actual needs identified by the people in partner countries.

CIDA

CIDA developed detailed guidelines for country programme, sector and project planning.[2] Its 1989 handbook – *Women in Development: A Sectoral Perspective* – put together available information to suggest ways to translate the agency's WID policy into actual programmes and projects. For each sector, the handbook briefly described the situation of women, including the constraints on their involvement, and identified the strategies needed to increase their participation. The second handbook – *Women in Development and the Project Cycle* – was again prepared as a quick reference for planners and project designers. It included guidelines on country programme planning, sector and project planning, project approach and implementation.

The guidelines on country programme planning included suggestions on country programme review, preparation of WID country profiles, WID country strategy, criteria for project analysis and selection, and sources of data. The guidelines on sector and project planning covered preparation of sector and project planning missions, sector analysis, project identification memoranda (PIM), logical framework and feasibility studies. Guidelines on project approval included project approval memoranda (PAM) and plan of operations or management plans (POP). Guidelines on implementation detailed suggestions regarding contracting, reporting, monitoring and evaluation.

Despite detailed guidance, there were 'gaps' between the guidelines and their actual use. For example, successive reports of the CIDA WID Steering Committee pointed out that gender issues were often considered too late in the process of programme/project development; that technical gender expertise was not sought early enough, and CIDA's development partners, particularly the Canadian executing agencies (CEA), had little gender expertise and commitment.[3] CIDA's WID policy assessment found similar limited use of the guidelines.[4]

UNDP

UNDP has issued a series of guidelines since 1975. Unlike NORAD, it did not establish targets and a timetable, but focused on 'how to' guidance like CIDA. In 1975 UNDP published a WID checklist.[5] In 1976 UNDP's *Guidelines on Project Formulation* included a section on women under 'special considerations'.[6] In 1977, UNDP developed more detailed programme guidelines on the integration of women in development.[7] It also issued a Programme Advisory Note (PAN) on WID.[8] In 1981 UNDP put out a supplement to the earlier guidelines focusing specifically on the data needs for planning for women.[9] After the creation of the WID division in 1987, UNDP developed a series of brief WID sector guidelines covering ten sectors. The guidelines were later incorporated in the *Programme and Project Manual* (PPM), again under the heading of 'special considerations' on projects.[10] As yet there is no internal assessment of the use and effectiveness of the guidelines. But UNDP's 1989 review of the implementation of its WID measures suggests that very little use was made of the guidelines. For example, during the previous country programming cycle (1987–91) 'advisory notes in only 4 field offices referred to gender issues'.[11]

The World Bank

Unlike the other donors, the World Bank did not issue any general or sector WID guidelines or checklists. Instead it produced sector-specific examples of 'best practices'. The sectors included Bank-identified priority sectors for women, such as agricultural extension, primary and secondary education, and forestry.[12] The Bank's 1994 policy paper on women promised to bring out operational tool kits about 'what to do' and 'what works' to facilitate discussion in various country environments.[13]

How effective were the guidelines as operational tools? Agency experiences suggest that guidelines were generally the first step. They set the standards and provided broad directions, but needed to be supplemented by other instruments, such as research, training and analytical tools. Additionally, in the absence of targets, timetables and accountability measures there was often no pressure to use the guidelines.

TRAINING

Training was identified by the donors as an effective instrument to raise awareness and expertise of agency staff on gender issues. CIDA and the World Bank prioritized training in the initial years of their WID programmes; in contrast, the UNDP and NORAD have only recently started staff training. Generally, agencies have focused on training their own staff, though some of the agencies (such as CIDA) have organized training of their development partners. CIDA also succeeded in putting most of its staff through WID training. In other agencies only a small fraction of staff was exposed to some type of WID/GAD training. In Tanzania and Bangladesh, NGOs and women's organizations have taken the initiative to organize WID/GAD training – the governments have only recently started training their staff in gender awareness.

Training methods and modules have evolved over the last two decades. Different agencies have used different models. For example, the World Bank and CIDA trained their staff mainly in what has now become known as the 'WID model' or the 'Harvard model' (because a group based at Harvard University developed the training module).[14] NORAD, in contrast, has followed the gender planning model, also known as the DPU model, developed by a group in the development planning unit of London University.[15] UNDP designed a more eclectic training methodology of its own. In the partner countries NGOs and women's organizations have generally emphasized women's empowerment approaches. Most of the agencies initially organized separate WID training, but later turned to integrated training, including gender issues in a wide variety of training topics.

Of the agencies, CIDA was the most successful in organizing systematic staff training. Training was one of the nine operational objectives of CIDA's WID action plan. By 1987 most of CIDA's regular professional staff had undergone the special WID training course. In addition, a limited number of staff were trained in the social/gender analysis course which was introduced later, in 1989. Gender issues were also integrated in the training of other topics, such as structural adjustment and human rights.[16]

NORAD, on the other hand, did not emphasize systematic staff training until 1989, though its WID action plan did recommend such a strategy. Only a small number of NORAD staff have completed the gender-planning training course, which has been introduced only in the last three years.

At UNDP, too, training was emphasized after the creation of the separate WID division in 1987. A 1989 review found less than 15 per cent of agency staff received WID/GAD training.[17] In 1990 UNDP recruited a full-time WID training coordinator, and the agency started building a cadre of WID trainers and a systematic programme of training.

Though the World Bank pioneered WID training in the early 1980s, staff training was deemphasized after the creation of the WID division in 1987. The Bank prioritized other strategies, such as research and country programming. In the last few years some of the regional WID coordinators in the Bank have started to highlight the importance of staff training to raise awareness and build expertise on gender issues. The Bank's 1994 policy paper on women recognized the importance of training and promised to put in place 'an intensive training program' to improve staff skills. The training is to raise awareness, as well as to provide tools and practical knowledge for policy and project design.[18]

In Bangladesh, NGOs such as BRAC, PROSHIKA, USHA and Banchte Shekha have developed innovative training methodologies. These have not yet penetrated the mainstream training institutions mandated to train public officials in development issues – the civil service training academy, rural development academies, and so on. The government has recently started gender training of public officials. However, the training is generally ad hoc and has been initiated mainly because of donor pressure.

The impact of training on changing agency operations is difficult to assess. There is a general impression within agencies that training has been more successful in raising awareness than in imparting expertise; that often junior women staff were the main participants in the training courses, though training should in fact have been targeted more at programme managers and corporate leaders.

A continuing dilemma of training is balancing the focus between training to extend knowledge and training to change attitudes. Many believe that training should aim at removing 'attitudes, values and fears that deny and are inhibitors to action'.[19] But changing deeply held personal biases is a time-consuming task, and many within agencies argue that a more feasible strategy is to change behaviour through incentives and disincentives, and limit training to imparting knowledge and expertise.[20]

How effective has training been in raising awareness and expertise? CIDA's evaluation of its WID policy found that about half of its professional staff received WID training. But the initial enthusiasm for WID training had tapered off by 1991. The new training course on social/gender analysis attracted only a small number of participants. CIDA's evaluation warned that one-shot training was inadequate to raise consciousness and expertise, and underscored the need to combine training with other instruments like research, analytical tools and so on. The evaluation found that though virtually all staff believed gender inequality to be a constraint, only about half believed it to be a serious one, and only one in three reported being knowledgeable about 'the general intent of CIDA's WID policy'.[21] Another recent study comparing the training experiences of several donors and national agencies emphasized the need to adapt training methods and modules to the needs of the audience, and argued that the impact of training – 'building skills, providing information, changing behavior and attitudes to gender issues' – could not be assessed over a short time and that a long-term perspective was needed.[22]

RESEARCH

Research, commissioned or funded by donors or conducted within the agencies, has played a significant role in making gender issues visible, and it continues to be a critical programming strategy. By generating quantitative and qualitative data, research has not only raised awareness about gender issues, but has been the basis of developing all other operational tools. Research has yielded gender-disaggregated data which have challenged many of the established paradigms and made a case for establishing alternative concepts and methods of data collection, analysis, training, and development planning and programming.

The data generated by research have marshalled powerful evidence about women's central role in economic development. Studies from around the world have shown that women's labour-force participation and economic contribution are vastly underestimated, particularly in agriculture and the informal sector, where women predominate;[23] that in some parts of the world, such as sub-Saharan Africa, family food production is primarily the women's responsibility;[24] that in the newly industrialized countries women constitute the bulk of the labour-force in the export-oriented industries;[25] that in many countries one-quarter to one-third of households are female-headed, and they tend to be the poorest of the poor;[26] that women's economic contribution in poor households is significant and they spend a greater proportion of their income and time in providing for the family's basic needs.[27] Research data have also indicated the constraints to raising women's productivity and returns – that women have unequal access to and control over productive resources (i.e. land, capital, education, training, market, information), organizations and decisionmaking bodies, which adversely affects the terms of their employment.[28]

All four donors emphasized research and disaggregation of data by gender as important programming tools. CIDA, NORAD and the World Bank prepared country-by-country WID profiles or situation analyses as part of their preparation of country WID/GAD strategy. The exercise involved the use of existing country statistics, supplemented by additional studies. The two bilateral donors – CIDA and NORAD – used OECD/ DAC's statistical reporting format on women-oriented assistance and required that management information on 'agents and beneficiaries' of projects be broken down by gender. UNDP and the World Bank, on the other hand, did not require such gender-disaggregated breakdown of management information. Donors used operational research to draw lessons about best practice in a wide variety of sectors, such as agricultural extension, credit, technology, natural resource management, and so on. Donors, especially the World Bank, focused on policy analysis to elaborate gender issues in sector and macroeconomic policies. Findings from theoretical research were also used to critique established concepts and models, and design alternative analytical tools.

In the partner countries, donors funded research on women. For example, in Tanzania NORAD's support to the university included funds for research on women in education, science and technology. In Bangladesh, NORAD funded research on a wide variety of topics, such as agriculture, donors' WID policies, politics and prostitution. As part of the Bangladesh agricultural sector review, UNDP funded a special study on women which brought to the attention of policymakers and planners valuable data on women's increasing role in field agriculture.[29] Similarly, the World Bank commissioned research on their priority sectors: credit, education and population.

Donor-funded research has uncovered a wealth of information over the past two decades, but most of it has tended to be confined to an ever growing body of WID/GAD specialists. Non-WID policymakers and programme and project personnel within agencies were only vaguely familiar with some of the research findings. Additionally, most of the research was supported by WID-earmarked funds. Donors were far less successful in addressing gender issues in the mainstream research projects which were carried out within the agencies or commissioned outside.

Though donor funding was critical in promoting research on gender issues in the partner countries, the lack of local institutional funds for research tended to make the research agenda in these countries donor-driven, and operational research took precedence over policy analysis and theoretical research. Donor emphasis on operational research created some imbalance between theoretical and operational research in partner countries. In the donor countries, research funds were available for both theoretical and operational research, the former being carried out primarily in the universities and the latter in the non-profit-making and consulting agencies. But in the partner countries, academic institutions lacked the institutional funds to support theoretical research and training on gender issues. As donor funding was mainly directed at operational research, the balance between theoretical and operational research was tilted in favour of the latter, so that the conceptual underpinning and institutional understanding of operational research remained weak.

SPECIAL PROJECTS

The initiation of special projects for women was one of the initial operational strategies pushed by the donors, and consequently by their development partners. The rationale for the special projects was to demonstrate on-the-ground approaches to overcoming obstacles to women's participation. Indeed, action projects, usually developed by NGOs, showed innovative approaches to reaching women and linking them with development resources, and indicated that investments on women yielded high social and economic returns.[30] Over the years, attempts were made to expand the scope of special women's projects from the social sector – health, population, family planning and nutrition – to the economic sector – agriculture, industry, energy, economic infrastructure, and so on. Income-generation and employment projects were designed which specifically targeted women. Projects were also developed to reduce women's unremunerated workload (the provision of cooking stoves, water and grinding mills, etc.) and hence to free their time for remunerated employment. There was a gradual progression from small-scale special women's projects to large multi-sectoral women's projects and women's 'components' in major sector or multi-sector projects.

In both Tanzania and Bangladesh a wide variety of special women's projects were promoted by the donors, as well as by the governments. Many of these projects had limited impact and influence, but a few were quite successful in reaching substantial numbers of poor women and in demonstrating innovative approaches. In Bangladesh, for example, nearly two million poor women were members of group-based credit programmes run by government as well as non-government initiatives (Grameen Bank, Swanirvar, BRAC, PROSHIKA, and so on). These programmes succeeded not only in creating assets and enhancing income, but also produced improvement on a number of social fronts, such as consciousness-raising, literacy, nutrition, health and family planning.[31] Targeted employment schemes, such as public work programmes, generated seasonal employment for nearly half a million destitute women annually in Bangladesh.[32] Many of these initiatives started small as pilot projects, but were later upscaled into major national programmes.

The successful projects yielded some 'how to' lessons for operations. For example, they demonstrated that often affirmative action policies were necessary to reach women – such as insistence on women's equal participation in projects, or starting first with women's groups. They showed that special measures were necessary to overcome class- and gender-based constraints. The measures included organization of separate women's groups for credit or separate women's crews in road work, provisioning of credit without collateral, services reaching women's doorsteps, and so on. In some situations, target specification was useful – such as Grameen Bank's insistence on landless groups. In all cases, building solidarity and organization through regular group meetings and providing access to and control over productive resources and services such as land, credit, training, technology, and market information proved to be essential. But the lessons from these successful initiatives were not widely disseminated, and they rarely informed policy dialogue during country programming exercises. For example, though grassroots organizing and participation was demonstrated to be critical in empowering women, only a few government and NGO initiatives adopted this strategy. Generally, governments and donors emphasized the welfare-oriented delivery-of-services approach more than the demand-oriented organizing and empowerment approach. Only in the last few years have donors become receptive to the idea of empowerment.

Despite the demonstrated success of a number of special projects and programmes, the special-projects approach to operations faced strong criticism. It was argued that instead of leading to replication and mainstreaming, the special projects were resulting in an alibi effect,[33] creating women's ghettos. Critics pointed out that the special-projects focus has deterred consideration of gender issues in macro- and sector-policy frameworks and in major programmes. However, many within donor agencies as well as in national governments believed that women-focused special projects would always be needed to facilitate the creation of a women's voice, autonomy and empowerment.

ANALYTICAL TOOLS

The donor agencies have developed a series of analytical tools to address gender issues in their operations. The most widely used tool was WID/GAD analysis for project appraisal, planning, monitoring and evaluation. The agencies used different names for their analytical tools; however, in most agencies WID/GAD analysis looked at several factors, such as gender-differentiated roles, gender-differentiated access to and control over resources, gender-differentiated needs, gender-differentiated obstacles and constraints, and gender-differentiated opportunities for participation. The agencies tended to highlight different elements, but generally they used a combination of approaches.

Canada and more recently Norway have integrated WID/GAD analysis in their project design and appraisal framework. At the UNDP gender-analysis tools are not integrated but are included in the Project Planning Manual (PPM) under 'special considerations'. The World Bank and the two countries have not yet introduced routine procedures to address gender issues in project design, appraisal, monitoring or evaluation.

Following the DAC/WID guidelines, the analytical tools of the two bilateral donors emphasized consultation with women and men of the target population in order to analyse gender needs and constraints, and to identify strategies to overcome obstacles to gender equity. The multilateral donors, by contrast, did not highlight consultation with the target population in their project design, appraisal or evaluation. Only recently have the multilateral donors started to pay attention to participation and consultation. NGOs in partner countries have, however, generally highlighted participation and the consultative process.

How effective have the analytical tools been in making agency operation gender-responsive? How widespread are their use? Data limitations make assessment difficult. Some have argued that since gender analysis and planning tools were designed primarily for projects with a 'target population', they are difficult to use when aid is not directly people-oriented. Yet such sectors of assistance – such as infrastructure, commodity aid, and emergency aid – constitute a majority of donors' development assistance packages. As donor agencies have shifted their attention in the last decade from simply meeting people's basic needs to encouraging partner countries to follow 'appropriate macroeconomic policies', the available tools, designed mainly for project analysis, were found to be of limited use in adapting to this shift from projects to policies.

COUNTRY PROGRAMMING

Country programming was identified by all the donors as one of the most promising strategies to mainstream gender issues. Generally, three instruments were used by donors to address gender issues in country programme exercises: preparation of WID/GAD country profiles; WID/GAD country strategy and action plans; and a package of WID components in major sectoral projects and programmes. NORAD, CIDA and more recently the World Bank have used all three in a systematic manner. Another instrument increasingly being used by donors is joint programming. In Bangladesh, for example, several donors have pooled together resources brokered by the World Bank to support long-term programme initiatives in the population and education sectors.

Following the recommendations of its 1985 WID strategy, Norway prepared WID situation analysis and country plans for all of its main partner countries. It also attempted to include women in country aid negotiations teams. CIDA prepared country WID/GAD strategies for 27 of the 150 countries receiving Canadian aid. The decision to decentralize CIDA operations made it easier to address gender issues in country programming, as it helped to access local conditions and local WID/GAD expertise. At the UNDP, again, approximately 37 per cent of country programmes addressed WID/GAD issues.[34] Since 1987, the World Bank, too, has started to emphasize country programming as a strategic entry point for addressing gender issues. In selected countries, such as Bangladesh, Pakistan, India and Kenya, the Bank prepared detailed situation analyses of women. This was followed by dialogue with partner governments and the preparation of major programmes in the Bank-identified priority sectors: education, population control and family planning, and agricultural extension.

The WID/GAD country strategies and plans prepared by the donors had mixed successes. The country WID/GAD profiles and situation analyses were useful for programme analysis. But separate country WID plans and strategies had limited influence in bringing about major changes in the country programme exercises. Indeed, WID country plans were often treated as annexes to the bilateral aid programmes rather than as guides to shape and change these programmes. For example, CIDA's WID evaluation found limited influence of WID country strategies on its bilateral programmes: only 14 per cent of bilateral staff reported that the CIDA WID country strategy and the general CIDA WID policy have had a major influence on their country programmes, and 33 per cent reported that there had been no significant influence.[35] UNDP's 1989 review found similar gaps. Though 41 per cent of country programmes during the previous programming cycle referred to WID issues, only nine country programmes actually translated this general reference into concrete programmes and projects.[36]

For Tanzania and Bangladesh the major instruments of national planning were the five-year and annual development plan exercises. Over the years, these plans have increasingly referred to WID/gender issues, in large measure due to donor pressure and incentive, and lobbying by women's groups. For example, in Bangladesh the five-year plans paid successively greater attention to women. The latest, fourth, five-year plan (1990–95) proposed eleven major strategies to achieve the objective of 'bringing women in the mainstream of development'.[37] The strategies included multisectoral programming; WID targets in sectoral programmes; gender-based human-resources planning; diversification of women's employment; increased credit facilities and skills training; and improvement of women's health, nutrition and productivity. The plan argued that different strategies were needed to bring the two groups of women – 'relatively poor' and 'relatively better off' – into the economic mainstream. For the poor, the plan proposed group-based strategies to raise consciousness of rights and to give access to and control over productive resources. For the relatively better off, it proposed increased opportunities in education and employment. The plan recommended the continuation of the quota system in public-service employment. Compared to the previous plans, the fourth five-year plan made a greater effort to mainstream gender issues in the discussion of the general as well as sectoral chapters of the plan document. But it did not establish any time-bound quantitative target to achieve gender equality; nor did it elaborate the institutional mechanisms and financial arrangements needed to implement the strategies identified in the plan.

Indeed, despite available quantitative figures of gender disparities, neither the donors nor their development partners made a realistic estimate of the financial cost of closing the gender gap. Similarly, donors and their partners did not explore innovative approaches to meet the cost of 'investing in women', though for other sectors different financial mechanisms were found. In Bangladesh, for example, the government has experimented with special levies to pay for special economic-sector projects. A special fee was imposed to support the construction of the Jamuna Bridge to link the north and south of the country; but no thought has been given to imposing similar taxes to finance special measures to enhance girls' education, or women's nutrition and health-care.

MACRO-POLICIES

In the last decade, donor assistance has increasingly shifted from projects to policies, largely due to the IMF's and the World Bank's focus on structural adjustment programmes (SAPs). At present SAPs constitute nearly a third of the total aid package. In the last few years research from around the world has highlighted the gender-differentiated impact of SAPs, and this has led donors and national governments to develop gender-aware approaches to structural adjustment.[38] One approach has emphasized measures to mitigate the adverse impact of SAPs, often through retargeting of public expenditure to poor women. Another approach has highlighted the barriers which gender relations create against the operation of adjustment measures (such as women's un-remunerated reproductive labour), and recommended public provisioning of childcare and care of the elderly, and supply of basic needs like water and fuel, to reduce market distortions. Often both strategies were adopted simultaneously, and donors, depending on their mandates, came forward with varying responses.

In recent years, the World Bank's structural adjustment lending to many countries included safety-nets for the poor, including women. The Bank's 1989 progress report noted that two of the eight fiscal structural adjustment operations in 1988 and three of the twelve fiscal operations in 1989 'set some conditions' or included 'some actions to help women contribute to macroeconomic adjustment or to improve their future productivity'.[39] Measures included nutrition programmes for pregnant and nursing women, healthcare for women and children, improving educational opportunities for girls in rural areas, training women in construction, and targeting credit to women. These were, however, largely palliative measures intended to soften the adverse impact, and did not challenge the basic directions of SAPs.

The debates surrounding the impact of SAPs generated interest in exploring the gender-differentiated impact of other macro-policies. How-ever, research is still at a rudimentary stage and only a few broad generalizations have been forthcoming. For example, it has been argued that the macro-policies of taxation, subsidies, public services and public employment can all have gender-differentiated impacts.[40] The burden of direct taxation may fall more heavily on men, since they participate more in formal-sector employment and earn a higher income; in contrast, the burden of indirect taxation may fall more heavily on women, as they disproportionately support the lower income households. Similarly, price subsidies on items such as food, fuel and basic drugs may differentially improve women's real purchasing power; on the other hand, subsidies on inputs to increase agricultural or industrial production may differentially benefit men, because of their greater access to and control of these productive sectors. Indeed, as research has earlier demonstrated, gender-blind policies to extend public services such as education, training, health, family planning, technology and extension have often had a gender-differentiated impact, because of public- and private-sector biases and the absence of specific measures to overcome gender-specific constraints on equal participation.

Donor agencies have started sponsoring research on macroeconomic policies from a gender perspective, and development partners have also increasingly raised gender issues in the context of macro-policies – structural adjustment, human resources development and poverty alleviation – but only a few innovative programming ideas have emerged so far. Giving priority to human development policies with a particular focus on gender equality is one of the promising programming ideas; promoting gender-responsive policies, particularly legal and institutional reforms, to remove barriers to women's equal participation – such as land ownership, access to credit and the market, and other factors of production and discrimination in the labour market – is yet another. However, further work on macro-policies is required before it is possible to draw firm conclusions about gender-responsive interventions.

POLICY DIALOGUE

As aid negotiations focused more on policy reforms, policy dialogues emerged as a key area for setting agendas. However, until now WID/gender issues have tended to be largely ignored in policy dialogues. There were two major constraints: first, the structure of representation in dialogue virtually ensured women's exclusion. Generally, policy dialogues were carried out between donors and partner governments; very few women had attained the senior decisionmaking level to represent either the donors or the partner government in the dialogue. Non-government groups and organizations, which were generally more effective in voicing gender issues, were not represented. Aid reviews and negotiations were on the whole conducted by men, with only the occasional presence of women; sometimes women were brought into the dialogues to discuss women-specific issues only. A second constraint was the structure of the development agenda itself. Policy dialogues generally dealt with macroeconomic and sector policies, and the relative paucity of relevant data regarding gender issues limited the debate on alternative policy options. During the dialogues concerns were often raised about the need to achieve gender equality, but the policy and programme implications of achieving such a goal were not systematically explored. As one WID advisor in a donor agency noted:

> Our country informed in advance about our WID/GAD priority, our delegation was headed by a woman who reiterated the priority in her opening remark. In response, the delegation of the partner country stated that it too placed high priority on women's participation, and there the dialogue on WID/GAD ended. Thereafter the country negotiations continued without any discussion about how the sectoral and country programming priorities might be reoriented given this high priority placed on WID/GAD issues by both the donor and partner countries.[41]

CIDA evaluation found that the agency had been least successful in addressing gender issues in policy dialogue and structural adjustment.[42]

SUMMARY

In the last two decades, donors have, through a process of trial and error, developed several strategies to make agency operations more gender-responsive. Research emerged early on as a critical strategy, as gender-disaggregated statistical data and analysis established the rationale for addressing WID/gender issues in public policy and development planning. Special projects and guidelines, the other initial operational strategies, were useful in demonstrating how alternative projects and programmes could be designed. But the special project approach in many cases tended to marginalize women, and guidelines were often ignored by programme and project managers.

In recent years donors have emphasized four instruments: country programming, training, macro-policies and policy dialogue. Since country programming was the major vehicle of donor assistance, addressing gender issues during country programme exercises was identified as a key mainstreaming strategy. Gender training gained in importance because it was believed that in order for operations to be gender-responsive, all staff needed to achieve gender sensitivity and expertise. The recent shift in focus from projects to policies has made identification of gender issues in macro-policies a potentially significant programming instrument, and raising gender issues in the context of policy dialogues has emerged as yet another promising mainstreaming strategy.

Over the past twenty years gender issues have certainly gained visibility and legitimacy in the donors' and national governments' development agenda, but the operational approach has fallen short in four critical areas. First, no serious attempt was made by the donors and the governments to identify clearly the core women's agenda and shape policy packages around that agenda. The pursuit of the goal of non-specific integration resulted in loss of focus on the core agenda. Second, donors and national governments did not pay sufficient attention to designing a financial plan to achieve a women's agenda. For example, though data about the gender gap in human development was well known, the donors and the national governments did not establish a budget to achieve gender equity. Third, donors and governments did not establish clear indicators to measure progress in achieving their WID goals, so that it was difficult to judge performance. Finally, the absence of women's voices in policy dialogues was another limiting factor.

From the beginning of the Decade, three key bars to achieving gender equality were highlighted by the women's movement – gender inequality in unpaid reproductive labour, in entitlement to factors of production, and in decisionmaking – but the donors and the governments have until now generally tinkered with these. They have yet to come forward with bold policies, adequate budgetary allocation and the institutional mechanisms to overcome the obstacles to women's equality.

NOTES

1. The Royal Norwegian Ministry of Development Cooperation (MDC), *Norway's Strategy for Assistance to Women in Development*, 1985.

2. CIDA, *Women in Development: A Sectoral Perspective*, 1989; CIDA, *Women in Development and the Project Cycle*, 1989.

3. CIDA, *Annual Report of the WID Steering Committee to President's Committee*, 1988–89, 1989–90, 1990–91.

4. CIDA, *Gender as a Cross Cutting Theme in Development Assistance: An Evaluation of CIDA's WID Policy and Activities 1984–1992*, July 1993.

5. Ester Boserup and Christina Liljencrantz, *Integration of Women in Development – Why, When, How*, UNDP, 1975.

6. UNDP, *Guidelines on Project Formulation* (G3400.2), 15 September 1976.

7. UNDP, *Program Guidelines on the Integration of Women in Development* (G3100-1/TL.1), 25 February 1977.

8. UNDP, *Program Advisory Notes Manual*, Chapter IX-1, 'Women in Development'.

9. UNDP, *Supplement 1 to UNDP Guidelines on the Integration of Women in Development: Activities Designed to Improve the Data Base for Planning for Women's Participation in Development* (G3100-1/TL.5), 14 September 1981.

10. UNDP, *Program and Project Manual*, February 1988.

11. UNDP, 'Analysis of the Field Office Response to Women in Development Questionnaire', mimeo, 1990.

12. The World Bank, *Women in Development: Issues for Economic and Sector Analysis*, working paper, August 1989; and Agusta Molnar and Gotz Schreiber, *Women and Forestry: Operational Issues*, working paper, May 1989.

13. The World Bank, *Enhancing Women's Participation in Economic Development*, 1994.

14. For a brief description of the different gender training methodologies, see Aruna Rao et al., eds., *Gender Training and Development Planning: Learning from Experience*, Population Council and Christian Michelsten Institute, 1992.

15. Personal interviews, 1991.

16. Personal interviews, 1991.

17. UNDP, *Women in Development: Report of the Administrator 1990*, p. 8.

18. The World Bank, *Enhancing Women's Participation in Economic Development*.

19. Rao et al., *Gender Training and Development Planning*, p. 62.

20. Ibid.

21. CIDA, *Gender as a Cross Cutting Theme*, p. 8.

22. Rao et al., *Gender Training and Development Planning*, p. 61.

23. Ruth Dixon, 'Women in Agriculture: Counting the Labour Force in Developing Countries', *Population and Development Review*, vol. 8, no. 3, pp. 539–66.

24. Barbara C. Lewis, ed., *Invisible Farmers: Women and the Crisis in Agriculture*, USAID, Washington DC 1981.

25. Guy Standing, 'Global Feminization through Flexible Labour', *World Development*, July 1989, pp. 1077–96.

26. Mayra Buvinic and Nadia H. Youssef with Barbara von Elm, *Women-Headed Households: The Ignored Factor in Development Planning*, USAID and ICRW Report, Washington DC 1978.

27. Meena Acharya and Lynn Bennett, *Women and the Subsistence Sector: Economic Participation and the Household Decision Making*, The World Bank, 1982; Daisy Dwyer and Judith Bruce, eds., *A Home Divided: Women and Income in the Third World*, Stanford University Press, Stanford 1988.

28. Ruth Dixon-Mueller, *Women's Work in Third World Agriculture*, ILO, Geneva 1985, pp. 25–33; Sherrie Kossoudji and Eva Mueller, *The Economic and Demographic Status of Female-Headed Households in Rural Botswana*, Population Studies Center, University of Michigan, Ann Arbor 1981.

29. UNDP, *Bangladesh Agriculture Sector Review*, vols. II and III, 1989.

30. Judith Tendler, 'What Ever Happened to Poverty Alleviation?', *World Development*, July 1989, pp. 1033–44; Anne Leonard, ed., *Seeds*, The Feminist Press, New York 1989.

31. Mahbub Hossain and Rita Afsar, *Credit for Women's Involvement in Economic Activities in Rural Bangladesh*, BIDS, Dhaka, December 1988.

32. Janet Jiggins, *Consultancy Report on Bangladesh*, mimeo, The World Bank, 1987.

33. Mayra Buvinic, 'Projects for Women in the Third World: Explaining their Misbehaviour, *World Development*, vol. 14, no. 5, 1986, pp. 653–64.

34. UNDP, *The Report of the Administrator 1990*.

35. CIDA, *Gender as a Cross Cutting Theme*.

36. UNDP, 'Analysis of the Field Office Response to Women in Development Questionnaire'.

37. Government of Bangladesh, *The Fourth Five-Year Plan, 1990–95*.

38. Diane Elson, 'Gender Issues in Development Strategies', paper presented at a seminar on Integration of Women in Development, Vienna, 9–11 December 1991.

39. The World Bank, *Women in Development: A Progress Report on the World Bank Initiative*, 1990, pp. 21–2.

40. Susan Joekes, Margaret Lycette, Lisa Macgowan and Karan Searle, 'Women and Structural Adjustment', mimeo, ICRW 1988; Susan Joekes, 'Gender and Macro Economic Policy', Institute of Development Studies, University of Sussex, mimeo, 1988.

41. Personal interviews, 1991.

42. CIDA, *Gender as a Cross-Cutting Theme*, p. 9.

CHAPTER 5

MEASURING PROGRESS

If a balance sheet were drawn up for women in the economy, it could be shown that women entered the labour force in large numbers, saw improvements in access to education in most regions, began to appear in sectors where they were previously absent, made up a slightly larger proportion of managerial and technical jobs. But it could also be shown that the rate of improvement in all of these indicators was slower than in the previous decade, that in terms of remuneration and conditions of work no aggregate improvement was registered, that women's unemployment rates tended to be higher, and that overall incomes declined. Poverty particularly afflicted families in which women are the sole income earners, a phenomenon that is growing.

The balance sheet on social conditions of women is similarly mixed. Improvements in legal conditions, in access to goods and services, such as education, have been registered. But increases in maternal and infant mortality in some developing countries have been observed for the first time in decades, as social services have been cut as part of adjustment packages.

The bottom line shows that, despite economic progress measured in growth rates, at least for the majority of developing countries, economic progress for women has virtually stopped, social progress has slowed, social well being in many cases has deteriorated, and because of the importance of women's social and economic roles, the aspirations for them in current development strategies will not be met.

1989 World Survey on the Role of Women in Development, United Nations, New York 1989, pp. 5–6

What has been the impact of the WID/GAD policies and measures implemented by the donor agencies and their development partners in the last two decades? Have they succeeded in bringing about a major shift in overall policy priorities, investment decisions and agency behaviour? More important, could one demonstrate that as a result of WID/GAD policies and instruments, progress has been achieved in improving women's condition and realizing the goal of gender equality? What are the measures of progress?

'Measurable progress' has become a debated issue within and outside agencies in the last few years. A concern with measurable progress arose in part because many of the bilateral donor agencies faced criticism from their taxpaying citizens about a lack of results. Critics argued that the 'aid business' bred corruption and waste on both sides – donors and aid recipients – and did not really benefit the intended 'target groups'.[1] To counter the critics, the donor agencies started talking about 'results–oriented' assistance, especially as their aid budgets were threatened with cuts by their parliaments. Quantitative figures – the numbers game – became an important sales pitch. As one of the heads of a donor agency stated:

> Grameen Bank is my favourite example. I can always defend our agency against the critics by arguing that we support initiatives like the Grameen Bank, which directly benefits a million poor women in Bangladesh. The taxpayers like to hear that kind of numbers![2]

Numbers and a sense of progress were important, not only for the survival of the aid business as a whole, but particularly for a new mandate like WID which had to compete with established programmes for limited agency resources. Though many of the big-budget established programmes like infrastructure and energy faced strong questioning of their relevance and efficacy from outside the agency, they did not have to struggle within their own agency for survival. Their ties with counterpart ministries and powerful lobbies in the partner countries were strong, and the 'demands' for assistance from the counterparts in these sectors were secure. In contrast, the small-budget WID programmes faced strong internal criticism. They could not demonstrate strong demand from the counterparts, and were under constant pressure to justify their existence. Indicators of progress were necessary for WID to counter their detractors within agencies.

Measures of progress were also needed to retain the support of the women's movement outside, which struggled in the first instance to put these WID programmes in place. Women's organizations, particularly those in the South, grew increasingly pessimistic about the state of progress. They pointed out that, despite considerable success in raising awareness and expertise in gender issues and increasing the number of WID projects and programmes, poverty and inequality continued to grow, as donors and their development partners failed to address their structural causes. Additionally, donors' preoccupation with WID institutionalization and special women's projects prevented them from adequately monitoring the gender impact of macro-policies – though in the final analysis it is these gender-blind macro-policies that were determining women's choices and opportunities. Women's networks from the South such as DAWN argued that the macro-policy instruments pushed by the donors in the 1980s, especially the structural adjustment programmes, resulted in a negative effect on gender equality: by cutting back on social-sector investment, especially in education and health, these policies were seriously undermining the realization of some of the key goals of the Forward Looking Strategies. The aim of these was by the year 2000 to eliminate illiteracy and to increase the life expectancy of all women to at least sixty-five years of good quality life.[3] Evidence from many countries, especially from South Asia and sub-Saharan Africa, indicated that progress in quality-of-life indicators had stalled.

What kind of information is available in the donor agencies and in the partner countries to measure progress? Until now donors have generated quantitative data in three areas: gender distribution of agency personnel, WID classification of budgets, and WID classification of projects. Data on these three elements were used to monitor the agency's progress in employing women, directing assistance to women and raising gender issues in agency operations, but the donors have not yet systematically assessed the impact of their assistance on improving women's condition and achieving gender equality in the partner countries. A part of the problem in measuring progress stemmed from the donors' failure to establish key indicators to track achievement of WID policy goals.

The partner governments also similarly failed to establish indicators to measure their progress. For example, gender-disaggregated data on several human development indicators – such as life expectancy, literacy, school enrolment, employment, nutrition and health, and public participation – indicated great disparities. But the partner governments generally did not use quantitative targets and incentives to close the gender gap in human development over a planned period. For example, the government of Bangladesh aggressively used quantitative targets and incentives to lower fertility rates and increase use of contraception, but it did not use similar techniques to improve conditions of women's lives in other areas – such as reduction of maternal and child mortality rates and the incidence of anaemia, and improvement in access to healthcare services. The planning documents, that is, the five-year plans, routinely made rhetorical pledges to achieve gender equality but they did not use results-oriented targets as planning and programming tools.

Assessment of progress thus has to be part quantitative and part impressionistic (see Figure 5.1). Here rough measures are used to gauge progress in achieving three major objectives: mainstreaming, gender equality and women's empowerment. To assess progress in mainstreaming, two broad indicators are used: mainstreaming resource and mainstreaming discourse. Personnel and budget data are analysed to see whether women are being mainstreamed in agencies' and governments' resources; public documents from donors and their partners are scrutinized to find out whether gender issues are gaining visibility and

Figure 5.1   Measures of Progress

Objective	Indicators
Mainstreaming	1. Resources • Personnel • Budget 2. Discourse • Visibility • Integration • Agenda-setting
Gender Equality	1. Law and Norms 2. Human Development
Women's Empowerment	1. Women's Movement 2. Public Action 3. Decisionmaking

transforming the development discourse. To assess progress in achieving the goal of gender equality, again two broad indicators are used: progress in both de jure and de facto equality, and in human development. Finally, to assess progress in women's empowerment, improvements along three indicators are analysed: strengthening the women's movement, women's increased participation in public action, and their presence in decision-making bodies.

MAINSTREAMING RESOURCES

WID advocates argued that since within agencies 'mandates ... whisper, service talks, money shouts',[4] it was necessary to increase the number of women staff and the WID budget. Generally a two-pronged strategy was favoured: a separate small core programme staff and budget for WID advocacy and catalytic work, as well as an increase in women's share in the agency's overall staff and budget. During the 1980s, most of the agencies succeeded in creating and maintaining a small WID-specific staff and budget, though these perpetually faced the prospect of withering away in the name of successful integration and main-streaming. The number of women staff in the agencies also registered

Table 5.1 The World Bank: Women in Professional and Management Job Categories (%)

Year	Job Category				
	Junior professional[a]	Senior professional[b]	Junior management[c]	Senior management[d]	Total
1976	n.a.	2.2	0.6	1.2	1.6
1985	17.1	6.4	3.0	1.2	12.5
1988	19.3	5.2	4.4	3.1	15.3
1990	21.0	10.7	6.2	2.7	16.1
1991	21.1	11.6	6.9	3.6	16.9
1992	23.1	13.2	7.9	6.5	16.1
1993	24.2	13.5	9.5	8.0	16.9

Notes: [a] Categories 22–23; [b] Categories 24–25; [c] Categories 26–27; [d] Categories 28 and above.
Source: The World Bank.

a slow and steady progress in the 1980s as a result of affirmative-action personnel policies. WID budget – WID-specific as well as WID-integrated – also increased gradually, though calculating WID budget was methodologically problematic.

Women's share of personnel

Personnel data from the four donor agencies indicate that women's share of jobs in professional categories improved slowly from approximately 20 per cent in 1975 to roughly 30 per cent in 1992–93 – a 10 per cent increase over twenty years! Generally, the greatest increase was in the category of junior and senior professionals; women's numbers in management positions, however, still remain low. On the whole, the bilateral donors have a better record than the multilateral organizations: by 1993, the two bilateral donors had achieved near-parity for women in professional categories, and approximately one-fifth of management positions in these agencies were filled by women. In contrast, by 1993 in the two multilateral organizations women constituted only around a quarter of the professional staff, and less than 10 per cent of management positions were occupied by women.

Of the four donors, the World Bank has the lowest percentage of professional and managerial women (see Table 5.1). Starting with a low base, women's representation at the Bank increased at a slow pace – from 12 per cent in 1985 to 16 per cent in 1993. Counting all job

Table 5.2   UNDP: Women in Professional and Management Job Categories (%)

Year	Job Category				
	Junior professional[a]	Senior professional[b]	Junior management[c]	Senior management[d]	Total
1975	46.5	14.7	6.8	3.0	20.6
1980	44.2	18.2	7.0	3.1	23.2
1986	35.7	18.0	7.8	5.5	22.3
1988	36.6	22.4	8.3	6.5	23.3
1990	38.7	24.6	8.7	8.3	26.2
1993	35.6	21.4	8.5	10.1	29.0

Notes: [a] Categories P1–P4; [b] Category P5; [c] Category D1; [d] Categories D2 and above.
Source: UNDP.

categories, women constituted 28 per cent of the Bank's employees. At senior management levels, women's share rose from 1 per cent in 1985 to 8 per cent in 1993. At junior professional levels it increased from 17 per cent in 1985 to 24 per cent in 1993. Women did not fare any better at UNDP (see Table 5.2). Women's share of professional and managerial jobs crawled from 20 per cent in 1975 to 29 per cent in 1993. In nearly twenty years, women's representation at senior management levels increased from 3 to 10 per cent, and in junior professional categories it actually declined from 46 per cent to 35 per cent. At the rate at which women's participation is increasing, it would take the World Bank and UNDP another half-century or more to achieve employment equity.

In contrast, by 1993, the two bilateral donors were close to achieving parity for women, at least in professional categories. NORAD has the highest percentage of professional women (see Table 5.3). Already in 1985, half of NORAD's professional positions were filled by women; two-thirds of junior professionals and a little over a quarter of senior professionals and junior managers were women. By 1992, the biggest change in NORAD was the significant increase in women's share of senior professional positions – from 28 per cent in 1985 to 43 per cent in 1992. Women's participation at senior managerial levels also rose – from 7 per cent in 1985 to 16 per cent in 1992; but there was a decline in junior management categories which resulted in a relatively static situation for women overall in management positions. Of all the donors, CIDA followed the most systematic approach of setting targets for each

Table 5.3 NORAD: Women in Professional and Management Job Categories (%)

Year	Job Category				
	Junior professional[a]	Senior professional[b]	Junior management[c]	Senior management[d]	Total
1985	75.4	28.0	30.0	7.7	50.6
1988	76.7	41.5	36.1	9.1	50.7
1991	77.9	43.3	39.1	8.7	50.0
1992	76.9	43.6	27.8	16.0	48.4

Notes: [a] Category V in Oslo and in field; [b] Categories III, IV and II in field; [c] Category II in Oslo; [d] Category I in Oslo and in field.
Source: NORAD.

Table 5.4 CIDA: Women in Different Job Categories (%)

Year	Job Category					
	Executive	Senior management	Scientific and professional	Admin and foreign service	Technical	Admin and support
1977	0	–	7.2	21.4	16.7	83.1
1981	2.6	–	5.6	28.3	16.7	85.3
1982	7.6	4.8	4.1	33.3	35.3	84.7
1983	8.9	6.3	6.9	33.9	47.4	86.0
1984	6.5	6.5	6.9	33.2	–	84.6
1985	8.1	10.2	8.3	37.8	45.0	87.6
1986	8.5	10.2	11.3	38.4	42.8	88.1
1987	10.6	10.6	7.3	37.6	44.4	87.8
1988	11.4	10.6	11.7	38.1	40.0	88.4
1989	14.1	10.8	11.2	39.8	42.8	89.5
1990	13.5	15.2	15.5	41.3	46.1	90.7
1991	14.4	18.6	15.2	43.7	46.6	90.5
1992	16.6	18.3	21.6	45.0	50.0	90.7

Source: CIDA.

Table 5.5 NORAD: Gender Distribution of Experts, 1985–91

Year	Experts	% Female
1985	217	4.1
1986	213	6.6
1987	205	8.3
1988	179	10.1
1989	154	8.4
1990	134	8.9
1991	97	10.3

Source: NORAD.

category of jobs, and it registered a steady progress in employment equity for all categories (see Table 5.4). In the fifteen years between 1977 and 1992 women's share of administrative and foreign service personnel more than doubled from 21 to 45 per cent; in technical categories it tripled from 16 to 50 per cent, and in executive and senior management positions it rose from no representation to 16 and 18 per cent respectively.

While women's share of regular staff positions registered gradual improvement, due largely to affirmative-action policies, their share of project-level expert positions and consultancies remained particularly low. For example, at NORAD, where women constituted nearly half of the professional staff, only 10 per cent of expert person years were served by women (see Table 5.5). Women's share rose from 4 per cent in 1985 to 10 per cent in 1991. But predictably women dominated in the lower ranks as volunteers (40 per cent) and as junior experts in multilateral organizations (43 per cent) (see Table 5.6). At CIDA, too, women's share of expert positions was much lower (27 per cent) than their share of professional positions, and remained virtually unchanged between 1985 and 1990 (see Table 5.7). At UNDP, between 1975 and 1980, women's share of project-level positions in fact declined, from 18 to 4 per cent, and then gradually increased to 20 per cent by 1993, a gain of mere 2 per cent in fifteen years (see Table 5.8). Systematic data about the gender distribution of consultancies are not available from agencies, but cursory information indicates women's low share. The 1989 UNDP internal review reported only 18 per cent of consultants to be women.[5] A recent World Bank survey noted not only gender gaps in recruitment of consultants, but also in conversion of long-term consultants to regular fixed-term appointments, and in salary level.[6]

Table 5.6 NORAD: Gender Distribution of Technical Assistance Personnel in Developing Countries

	Person years		Women person years		% women	
	1990	*1991*	*1990*	*1991*	*1990*	*1991*
Under bilateral agreements	275	222	69	61	25	27
Experts in main partner countries in Africa	131	93	11	10	8	10
Experts in main partner countries in Asia	4	4	1	0	25	
Volunteers	140	125	57	51	40	40
Junior experts in multilateral organizations	35	37	15	16	42	43
Total person years	310	259	84	77	27	29

Source: NORAD.

Personnel data from the agencies indicate some common patterns. Despite improvements in the last two decades, the pyramidal pattern of women's representation – concentration at the bottom and declining presence at higher grades – still holds for all the agencies. The improvement in women's participation in field positions, either as regular staff or as experts, is much slower than in headquarters jobs; women's representation is also particularly low in senior management categories.

The slow pace of progress, especially in the multilateral organizations is attributed to a variety of factors. A World Bank report pointed out that the Bank's image as 'a bastion of male privilege' and 'old-boys' network' makes the Bank a hostile and unpromising place for women to have a successful career.[7] In a staff survey conducted in 1988, '73 per cent of the women viewed the Bank's working environment as non-supportive'.[8] The women working at UNDP shared similar feelings about male control of managerial positions and networks, and argued that women lacked 'godmothers' to lend the support and networking contacts which male colleagues could take for granted from male 'godfathers'.[9]

In recent years, both the Bank and the UNDP have taken special measures to recruit women for management-level positions. The UN secretary-general has issued a directive to bring about gender parity in management-level positions by 1995. The World Bank has recruited a

Table 5.7   CIDA: Share of Women among Experts Abroad, 1985–90

Sectors	1985	1986	1987	1988	1989	1990
Agriculture	13.6	13.5	27.3	19.7	15.0	16.7
Education	36.3	38.9	37.6	32.8	35.5	35.2
Economic and financial support	19.1	–	–	–	18.4	19.3
Energy	3.8	2.9	1.9	1.9	1.1	3.9
Environment	–	–	23.0	–	33.3	27.9
Communications	39.1	15.5	3.5	14.7	13.8	25.9
Fisheries	11.2	9.1	12.9	9.8	9.3	12.5
Forestry	7.9	8.4	6.1	6.3	12.6	9.1
Geological survey	3.9	10.0	0	17.1	5.4	7.1
Health and nutrition	59.5	60.3	60.7	59.3	57.8	57.8
Human resources development	–	–	–	–	44.8	58.1
Industry	3.1	6.2	14.7	9.2	9.1	13.7
Institutional support and management	27.7	–	21.1	18.7	26.0	23.4
Material management	22.2	–	–	–	20.0	16.7
Mining and metallurgy	13.1	1.8	43.5	3.2	1.3	3.9
Multi-sector	–	–	17.3	37.1	25.4	17.9
Population and human settlement	51.9	46.5	37.3	54.9	41.0	38.2
Transportation	5.1	2.3	3.7	1.5	3.4	3.0
Water and sanitation	2.1	4.9	8.4	7.0	9.2	11.5
WID	–	–	97.2	–	88.9	89.6
Not specified	–	–	35.3	50.0	50.0	–
Other	–	–	21.1	37.1	0	–
Total	27.9	26.1	28.3	24.6	25.4	27.7

Source: CIDA.

special WID advisor in the personnel department to push for an acceleration of women's recruitment and promotion in the Bank. There are, however, some built-in constraints. Instead of looking at places like non-government organizations, where many capable women are to be found, agencies generally look for women in the governments or banks, where few women have thrived. Very few women have worked at senior levels in national bureaucracies to enable them to get the 'blessings' of their governments to be nominated for senior positions in multilateral agencies. Additionally, UNDP and the Bank have not yet adopted gender-responsive career-development policies – such as flexible maternity-leave

Table 5.8 UNDP: Women in Project-Level Job Categories, 1975–90 (%)

	Junior Professional[a]	Senior Professional[b]	Junior Management[c]	Senior Management[d]	Total
			Job Category		
1975	30.0	20.0	14.3	0	18.5
1980	9.4	2.3	2.4	0	4.7
1986	23.3	9.6	0	0	14.4
1988	28.8	10.1	1.9	0	18.9
1990	31.0	9.4	6.7	0	20.3
1993	26.7	21.8	0	0	20.3

Notes: [a] Categories L1–L4; [b] Category L5; [c] Category L6; [d] Category L7.
Source: UNDP.

Table 5.9 WID in Norway's Development Assistance

	1988	1989	1990	1991
WID as % of total Norwegian aid				
Total WID	18.2	18.4	16.1	21.1
of which:				
WID-specific	1.1	1.8	1.5	1.4
WID-integrated	17.1	16.6	14.6	8.4
WID-relevant	–	–	–	11.3
WID as % of total bilateral aid				
Total bilateral WID projects	22.6	22.0	18.2	25.6
of which:				
WID-specific	1.8	3.0	2.4	2.1
WID-integrated	20.8	19.0	15.8	10.0
WID-relevant	–	–	–	13.5
WID as % of total multilateral aid				
Total multilateral WID projects	14.3	15.2	14.1	16.3
of which:				
WID-specific	0.5	0.4	0.4	0.4
WID-integrated	13.8	14.8	13.7	6.9
WID-relevant	–	–	–	9.0

Source: NORAD.

Table 5.10   CIDA: WID Involvement and Budget by Sector, 1990–91 (%)

Sector	WID Involvement	WID Budget
Agriculture	65	12
Education	47	23
Energy	20	19
Fisheries	50	2
Forestry	43	38
Health and nutrition	60	78
Population and human settlements	57	34
Mining and metallurgy	0	0
Communications	25	1
Transportation	25	1
Water and sanitation	67	34
Geological survey	0	0
Food Aid	0	16
Industry	100	12
Institutional support and management	46	22
Material management	0	0
Economics and financial support	17	15
Human resource development	73	44
Total	43	20

Source: CIDA.

provisions, flexitime for staff with childcare responsibilities or who care for elderly relatives, concurrent reassignment of career couples in the same duty station, assistance with spouse employment in the field, and so on. Since the terms and conditions of employment do not accommodate women's productive as well as reproductive roles, it still remains difficult for women to have 'successful careers' in agencies which require that 'staff members rotate between geographical locations, different functions and occupational groups and through increasing levels of responsibility'.[10]

While WID advocates within agencies have emphasized women's share of agency posts as an indicator of mainstreaming, the feminists in the women's movement, particularly from the South, have pointed out the limitations of simple body counts, arguing that advancing women's careers and advancing the women's agenda within agencies were two different objectives; there might not be a strong link between the two. Having more women professionals and managers would not necessarily result in making the agencies operationally more gender-sensitive. Indeed, many of the women professionals and managers might be just as

Table 5.11 WID Support as % of Total Sector Support in Norway, 1988–91

Sector	1988	1989	1990	1991
Multilateral assistance	12	15	14	15
Planning and public administration	5	4	46	35
Water and energy supply, transport, communications	23	27	12	15
Agriculture and fishing	15	12	19	38
Industry, oil, mining, handicraft	17	1	1	3
Banking, finance, tourism	84	69	83	74
Education, science	11	17	14	33
Health, population	55	44	29	54
Social infrastructure	14	22	53	61
Rural development	36	41	51	90
Environment	6	4	15	22
Women's projects, not referable to sector	94	98	99	100
Not referable to sector	3	x	x	1
Unspecified	3	4	7	10

Note: x = less than 1%.
Source: NORAD.

ignorant of or hostile to the 'women's agenda' as their male colleagues. Additionally, many of the women managers might feel the pressure to distance themselves from the 'women's agenda'. The feminists from the South also pointed out that if career advancement of women was to be an indicator of progress, then multilateral agencies needed to adopt special measures to identify Southern women candidates, who were particularly underrepresented in the agencies.

WID assistance

The two bilateral donors, following OECD/DAC/WID's statistical classification format, reported their WID assistance, which amounted to approximately 20 per cent of their development assistance, most of which was 'WID-integrated'. The two multilateral agencies, by contrast, did not adopt any statistical reporting format for their WID budget, and hence it was not possible to calculate their WID assistance. In both NORAD and CIDA social sectors have generally fared better in mainstreaming WID assistance, though some of the economic sectors such

Table 5.12　NORAD: Special Grants to Various Sectors, 1988–91
(million kroner)

	1988	1989	1990	1991
Environment	39.1	69.7	66.6	78.5
Women	23.1	27.9	31.5	32.7
Culture	9.7	12.6	12.1	10.3
Technical assistance	28.1	20.2	14.9	20.1
Aids	–	–	65.8	72.1
Total	100.0	130.4	190.9	213.7

Source: NORAD.

as rural development and banking in NORAD appear to have a fair amount of success at mainstreaming resources. Surprisingly, education and agriculture, two sectors of vital importance for women, have not made much progress in increasing WID assistance in either of the two agencies.

Though both NORAD and CIDA reported WID assistance using the fourfold DAC classification criteria (i.e. women from the aid-recipient country must be consulted and given active participation; WID expertise must be utilized; and barriers to female participation must be identified and measures introduced to overcome them), each introduced for internal purposes an additional category to broaden the scope of WID classification. For example, since 1991 NORAD has started using a new category – 'WID-relevant assistance' – which counted projects that fulfilled one or more of the four OECD/DAC criteria. Similarly CIDA used a separate classification of 'WID involvement' as opposed to 'WID budget' for projects.

Predictably there was a gap between the OECD/DAC classification category and the additional categories. For example, at NORAD in 1991 nearly 10 per cent of aid could be classified as WID assistance using all four DAC criteria, but an additional 11 per cent could be classified as WID-relevant (see Table 5.9). At CIDA, while only 20 per cent of assistance could be classified as WID, nearly 43 per cent of operations could be classified as having some 'WID involvement' (see Table 5.10). At CIDA the disparity between 'WID involvement' and 'WID budget' was most glaring in some of the economic sectors. For example, in agriculture, 65 per cent of the operations could be classified as having WID involvement but only 12 per cent had WID budget.

Similarly in industry (100 per cent WID involvement, 12 per cent WID budget), fisheries (30 per cent WID involvement, 2 per cent WID budget), and transport and communication (25 per cent WID involvement, 1 per cent WID budget), the gap between WID involvement and WID budget was great. Surprisingly, in a few of the economic sectors, such as energy, forestry, and economic and financial support, the gap between WID involvement and WID budget was narrow.

At CIDA, generally, the social sectors fared better in mainstreaming WID assistance. The five sectors with the highest proportion of WID budget were health and nutrition (78 per cent), human resources development (44 per cent), forestry (38 per cent), water and sanitation (34 per cent) and population and human settlements (34 per cent). At NORAD, by contrast, some of the economic sectors have succeeded more than the social sectors in mainstreaming WID (see Table 5.11). For example, the five sectors with the highest properties of WID budget at NORAD were rural development (90 per cent), banking and finance (74 per cent), social infrastructure (61 per cent), health and population (54 per cent), and agriculture and fishing (38 per cent).

Following the model of the OECD/DAC WID statistical classification, the two bilateral donors have also attempted to classify their environment assistance. Up to now a higher percentage of assistance in both agencies can be classified under WID. At CIDA, during 1990–91, 20 per cent of assistance could be classified under WID and 13 per cent under environment. Similarly at NORAD in 1991, 1,617 million kroner could be classified as WID assistance and 1,361 million kroner as environmental assistance.

While a greater proportion of assistance can be classified under WID, agencies have generally allocated a much smaller specific WID budget. For example, in NORAD special WID funds are less than half the size of the special environment funds, and the special Aids grant (see Table 5.12). It is interesting to note that though a concern with the environment emerged within agencies much later than WID, the agencies started their environmental work with a much greater financial allocation than they did with WID. Environmental mandates, like WID mandates, were created because of outside political pressures. But agencies responded much more seriously (measured in terms of staff and budget) to environmental lobbies than to WID lobbies.

As with women's share of personnel, the use of the WID budget as an indicator of progress faced some criticism. The protagonists argued that since in the final analysis it is the budget that defines priorities and commitment, a WID budget classification is a powerful monitoring tool in the hands of managers within agencies and government: an increased share of assistance indicates the agency's commitment to WID. But the critics pointed out the imperfections of the methodology – that a large portion of the aid budget was not people-oriented and hence fell outside the purview of the WID budget classification. They also argued that a simple money count, like the body count in personnel, did not give any idea about the progress of the women's agenda. An increase in WID budget did not necessarily imply a qualitative change either in sectoral priorities or in development paradigms. Often an increased WID budget was the result of an expansion of 'WID components' within the existing policy and project framework.

MAINSTREAMING GENDER ISSUES IN DEVELOPMENT DISCOURSE

Early in the Decade, WID advocates identified invisibility and marginalization as major barriers to women's equality. In the 1950s and 1960s, development literature and agency documents simply did not refer to gender differentials. It was assumed that men and women benefited equally from development.

Research and action projects initiated around the world in the 1970s found increasing evidence of gender-differentiated contributions to and benefits from development. The new data called into question some of the basic assumptions on which development theories and planning models were based. However, the mainstream development discourse did not readily welcome the new data and evidence generated by the women-focused research, micro-surveys and projects, and the new information was largely circulated within the narrow field of WID.

Visibility

Gaining visibility and avoiding marginalization thus became a key concern of WID advocates. Within agencies, a conscious strategy was adopted to make gender issues as visible as possible in agency documents. Visibility as well as integration was sought through multiple means: separate WID reports or sections in agency reports, raising gender issues in macro- and sectoral policy discussions; pictorial display of women in productive activities; case studies highlighting 'success stories' of working with women, and so on. As a result of these multi-pronged efforts, gender issues have become increasingly visible in donor agency documents over the past two decades. The annual reports of the donors have generally included a separate WID section, and increasingly the donors made an effort to raise gender issues in macro- and sectoral policy discussions. WID/GAD was accorded the status of a priority theme by at least three of the four donors: NORAD, CIDA and UNDP. The use of women's photographs and case studies of women's initiatives grew dramatically in agency publicity materials. Indeed, it often appeared that poor women from the South were rendered visible in order to sell 'development' in the same way that glamorous women models are used to sell commercial products.

Any assessment of progress in mainstreaming gender issues within agency discourses has to be largely impressionistic, as there is very little quantitative data comparable to the data on staffing and budgets. Some donors have attempted to count 'treatment' of gender issues in agency discourses. For example, the World Bank reported progress in attention to gender issues during 1988–89 compared to the previous eight years, after reviewing the 'treatment of women' in its economic and sector work. The Bank reviewed 254 economic and sector reports prepared in 1988 and 1989, and found that 25 per cent of them addressed 'women's issues' in some detail. In comparison, only 19 per cent of reports in a sample covering the years 1980–87 addressed women's issues.[11] Women's issues were discussed primarily in the Bank-identified high-priority sectors: population, health and nutrition, education and agriculture.

The majority of reports discussed 'women's issues in the context of family planning, maternal and child health, safe motherhood, nutrition, and school enrollment'.[12] Some emphasized the role of women as agents in the reduction of poverty or as actual or potential producers. The Bank's review noted that women's roles had 'not been addressed as often in reports on small and cottage industries, energy, urban development, or rural transport, all fields in which the participation of women can be significant'.[13]

Other donors did not attempt to monitor the treatment of gender issues in the agency documents and publications. But impressionistic assessment from the UNDP's various reports, particularly annual reports to the Governing Council and annual publications such as the *Human Development Report*, again, indicate growing visibility and recognition of gender issues in the agencies' discourse. For example, the UNDP's annual reports to the Governing Council between 1975 and 1987 referred to WID/GAD issues only in the years when the three UN Women's Conferences were held – 1975, 1980 and 1985! Though each year's report discussed major developmental issues of the day, no attempt was made to raise gender issues in these discussions. UNDP started regularly reporting on its WID activities after the establishment of its WID division in 1987, but discussion of gender issues remained generally restricted to the separate WID section and did not spill over to the other development issues discussed in the annual report. Only once – in the 1989 report – were gender issues discussed under the theme of human development.[14]

Over the years in all agency documents gender issues have gained visibility and sectoral policy debates have increasingly become gender-sensitive. The most significant progress was in the recognition of women's economic roles and contributions. Three decades ago, in the donors' development discourses, women were portrayed only in their reproductive roles, as mothers and as a disadvantaged group needing welfare benefits. But now women's growing responsibilities as the sole or primary income-earners in their families are openly acknowledged. Data about female-headed households, showing that between a quarter and a third of households are headed by women, have gained visibility. Women's roles in agriculture and in providing household food security are by now well documented.[15] There is open acknowledgement that donors' policies and practices, by ignoring women's roles in agriculture and targeting resources to men, have contributed to economic disasters, particularly in Africa. Women's contributions, especially in manufacturing and export-oriented industries, have also drawn widespread attention in recent years.[16] Women's roles in various economic sectors – such as macro-enterprises, energy, infrastructure, urban and rural development, employment, and natural resources management – have similarly gained acceptance within agencies.[17]

Integration

To avoid marginalization, WID advocates within agencies have attempted to integrate discussion of gender issues under relevant sections of agency documents. Again they have gained some success. For example, in addition to the mandatory WID section, NORAD's 1988–89 aid review presented to OECD/DAC discussed gender issues in only two other places: under discussion of 'natural resources and environment' and 'aid for energy'.[18] The aid review for 1990–91, on the other hand, mainstreamed discussion of gender issues throughout the report under each sector: agriculture, rural development and food security; energy; health and population; and natural resources management and environment. WID was listed as one of the six priority areas of assistance.[19]

CIDA's reports to OECD/DAC indicated similar attempts to mainstream gender issues. For example, its 1988–89 aid review, in addition to the WID section, referred to gender issues under the sectoral theme of agriculture, rural development and food security; identified WID as one of the six priority themes of assistance; and noted that 35 per cent of projects met all WID requirements – an improvement from the previous year, when 24 per cent of projects met such requirements.[20]

UNDP's annual publication, the *Human Development Report*, consistently mainstreamed gender issues in discussion. The creation of the gender-disaggregated human development index and presentation of gender-disaggregated human development data had been a very imaginative tool to measure progress towards gender equality. In contrast, the World Bank's annual development reports had not made any effort to highlight gender issues in the discussion. For example, the *World Development Report* of 1992, which focused on the environment, completely ignored women's roles in natural resource management.[21]

Agenda-setting

There was also slow progress towards agenda-setting. In the last two decades, social-sector analysis, which had traditionally highlighted women's concerns, turned more consciously towards an agenda-setting approach. The exclusive focus on women as mothers gradually shifted to a human-development and human-rights perspective. In the population sector, for example, agency preoccupation with limiting women's fertility slowly gave way to a concern for their reproductive health and reproductive rights. The importance of gender relations and male responsibility gained slow recognition. In the health sector, concern with maternal health was expanded to include the other health needs of women. Similarly, education-sector planning became more sensitive to the complex nexus of factors – poverty, household discrimination, lack of facilities – that contribute to continued gender disparities. Gender-based discrimination issues such as women's human rights, violence against women and sexual harassment became legitimate concerns of donor agencies.

However, it is not clear how much of the shift simply reflects a change in agency language and how much has been actually operationalized. Indeed, in recent years the donors have been very adept in coopting the language of feminists and the women's movement. Agency documents frequently use such terms as empowerment, participatory development, self-determination, autonomy, self-reliance, choice, and voice, which were coined and used by feminists. But it is hard to gauge from the shift in agency language how much change has taken place in agency operations. Evidence from field-level assessment is needed to judge whether the changes in agency language reflected only rhetorical shifts or implied real changes in policies, programmes and investment. For example, the United Nations Population Fund (UNFPA), which for years emphasized population control and viewed women as the passive recipients of family planning programmes, recently shifted its language and started to talk of women's 'self-determination' and 'investing in women'. But it is far from clear how much of this shift in language has actually been translated operationally into alternative policy and pro- gramme design. Available evidence suggests very little change in oper- ations. The cooptation efforts of some agencies are even more blatant: for example, the United Nations Children's Fund (UNICEF) talks about 'empowering' women to breastfeed babies!

In the last two decades agency discourses have slowly embraced evidence from research and action projects about women's actual and potential economic contributions; but their policy debates and prescrip- tions have not yet given commensurate weight to removing gender- specific barriers to women's equal participation. For example, data about women's involvement in reproductive labour and its constraining impact on women's participation in productive activities were readily acknowl- edged, but public policy options to underwrite the cost of reproductive labour were never seriously investigated by the agencies. Donors as well as their development partners encouraged women to increase their participation in productive activities, and indeed poverty and growing family responsibilities pushed an increasing number of women into waged employment. But very little relief was forthcoming from donors and governments in reducing the load of women's reproductive activities – care of children, the elderly and the sick; provisioning of basic needs such as food, fuel and water – which was largely left to private arrange- ment and continued to fall disproportionately on women. Indeed, the development strategies promoted in the 1980s, whether by the multi- nationals or by the World Bank and the International Monetary Fund (IMF), relied heavily on cost-cutting measures, primarily reducing social safety nets for workers and social-sector investments. These strategies completely ignored the major lessons that WID/gender advocates had learned in the previous decade: that the promotion of gender equality depends on increasing investment in women's education, health and nutrition; that women's productive and reproductive labour are inter- twined, and an increase in productive labour without reducing the burden of reproduction would only result in decreasing women's and children's wellbeing.[22]

The donors not only underemphasized the issue of cost of repro- ductive labour; they also did not focus on some of the other key gender- specific constraints. For example, lack of property rights, particularly the right to inherit agricultural land, has long been identified as a major obstacle to improving women's productivity and participation, yet donors did not push vigorously for land reforms, and reforms in inheritance laws in particular. Up to now, donors have primarily chosen to prioritize support for pilot employment projects and programmes giving women access to land, forests and credit, but they have not pushed for policy reforms to give women equal rights to inherit land, receive credit and become members of cooperatives.

Lack of voice in setting their own agenda and the national development agenda was highlighted as yet another major obstacle to women's equal participation. Women's groups, particularly in the South, emphasized the need for participation and empowerment, but these ideas took a long time to find entry into the donors' discourses.

GENDER EQUALITY

What has been the progress in the partner countries? Have Bangladesh and Tanzania achieved significant improvement in women's development in the last two decades? To assess progress towards the goal of gender equality, two indicators can be used: law and norms, and human development.

Law and norms

As noted earlier, the constitutions of both Bangladesh and Tanzania recognize women's equal rights. But the laws relating to marriage, divorce, child custody and property inheritance are still being governed by customary or community religious laws which discriminate against women and limit women's rights to exercise their choices and participate in development. In the last two decades very little progress has been made in reforming the personal laws in the two countries.

Bangladesh has ratified UNCEDAW, but with reservations on Articles 2, 13(a) and 16 which concern women's equals rights in the family. The laws concerning adultery and citizenship are also discriminatory towards women. In situations where laws have been enacted in Bangladesh – for example, the Dowry Prohibition Act of 1980 and cruelty to women (Deterrent Punishment) Act of 1983 – enforcement has been slow, which made these laws largely ornamental and not active vehicles of social change. Indeed, lack of awareness and enforcement have remained major obstacles to women's exercising even their limited rights in divorce, maintenance support, child custody and other such matters.

Over the years social norms have changed, but they still remain a major barrier to women's equal participation. A survey conducted in Bangladesh in 1993 found that while 40 per cent of women identified lack of opportunities as a barrier, 28 per cent found social and religious customs and norms to be the obstacles to their participation in income-earning activities.[23] Additionally, the norms have changed more in order to accommodate women's enhanced economic responsibilities than to support more equal gender relations. For example, in Bangladesh the norm of *Purdah* (female seclusion) has been gradually eroded in the last two decades because poverty has pushed a growing number of women to find employment and income outside the home. But the changing norm regarding *Purdah* has not necessarily changed gender roles in unpaid reproductive labour or in gender relations.

Human development

In the last two decades in both Tanzania and Bangladesh there has been progress in human development, but the progress is greater in Tanzania than in Bangladesh. For example, in the last twenty years, female enrolment in schools has improved much more in Tanzania than in Bangladesh. During the period 1970 to 1985–87 in Tanzania, the ratio of female to male enrolment increased at first level from 65 to 100, and at second level from 40 to 62. In Bangladesh, by contrast, it increased from 47 to 66 at first level, and reached only 39 at second level. However in Bangladesh, the female ratio of enrolment at third level (24) was higher than in Tanzania (16). Similarly, health indicators show greater progress in Tanzania: female life expectancy increased by 9 years during 1970 to 1990, and at 54 years was 3 years more than male life expectancy. In Bangladesh, on the other hand, though female life expectancy increased by 8 years, at 50 years it was lower than male life expectancy – one of the few countries going against the global norm of a higher female life expectancy. Maternal and child mortality rates remained high for both countries, though Bangladesh's (600) was double that of Tanzania (340). In Tanzania, 60 per cent of births were attended by trained personnel, compared to only 5 per cent in Bangladesh.[24] Additionally, between 1970 and 1990, the fertility rate dropped in Bangladesh from 7 to 5 per cent while in Tanzania it increased from 6 to 7 per cent. The increase in women's labour-force participation rate (4.4 per cent) was higher than men's (2.5 per cent) in Bangladesh; while the reverse was the case in Tanzania (2.6 per cent for women, 3.2 per cent for men).[25] But in Bangladesh the higher economic participation rates were mostly poverty-induced, and economic opportunities opened for women largely in insecure, casual, female-stereotyped low-income jobs. On average, women's income remained less than men's: wage rates for female day-labourers were less than half those of males. Available data from Tanzania indicate a similar concentration of women in low-waged jobs. In Tanzania, progress in women's participation in public life (13 per cent of decisionmaking jobs and 16 per cent of ministerial-level positions) is comparable to that of many of the donor countries, for example Canada (6 per cent of decisionmaking jobs in all ministries and 17 per cent of ministerial-level positions). By contrast, in Bangladesh, the rates of women's participation (3 per cent of decisionmaking jobs and 2 per cent of ministerial-level positions) is dismal.[26] What explains the relative differences in achievements in human development between Tanzania and Bangladesh?

Disparities in policies

Though the per-capita gross national product (GNP) of Tanzania (US$110) was lower than that of Bangladesh (US$210), the greater progress in Tanzania in women's education and health was due to macro- and social-sector policy differences between the two countries, rather than their WID policy differences. Tanzania gave higher priority to social-sector investment during the 1960s and 1970s, which resulted in higher levels of human development indicators for both men and women. In Bangladesh social-sector investment received lower priority: during the period 1973–80, 11 per cent of development expenditure was allocated to social sectors; during the second (1980–85) and third (1985–90) five-year plan periods, 12 per cent and 10 per cent respectively of the development budget were spent on social sectors. Women were primary targets in only two of the social sectors – population control, and family planning and women's affairs – and direct allocation for women remained less than 0.3 per cent of the total public-sector development budget.[27]

The influence of national government and donor policies on women's lives was felt most strongly in Bangladesh only on two indicators – female fertility rate and contraceptive prevalence rate. An analysis of donors' resource-allocation patterns indicates the high priorities they attached to controlling women's fertility. Women's health and education, by contrast, received a lower priority. According to one estimate, between 1980 and 1986, about 19 per cent of project allocations (US$844 million out of US$4400 million) went to projects where women were the sole or part of the target group.[28] Of these, 55 per cent went to population and family planning projects, and only 2 per cent to health and 8 per cent to education. Thus, despite insignificant progress registered in women's education, health, nutrition and other indicators of development, fertility rates declined and the contraceptive prevalence rate increased significantly in Bangladesh.

The relative success in Bangladesh of affecting fertility rates through public policy intervention – i.e. population control policy and family planning programmes – raises the question: how seriously have the donors and the government pursued a gender equity policy, or for that matter a policy of women's welfare? If measurable and significant results were achieved in fertility decline and contraceptive use, why was there no comparable progress in other measures of women's health and education, such as nutritional intake, maternal and child mortality, literacy and school enrolment?

Indeed, data indicate a continuation of the gender gap in these aspects. Between the two nutrition surveys of 1975–76 and 1981–82, adult males increased their calorie intake, while adult females suffered an actual decline.[29] The incidence of chronic long-term malnutrition (57 per cent for women; 54 per cent for men) and acute malnutrition (9 per cent for women; 6 per cent for men) continued to remain higher among women.[30] The maternal mortality rate has remained relatively unchanged over the last two decades, and accounted for nearly 27 per cent of all female deaths.[31] Gender differentials in the child mortality rate (16 girls per thousand, compared to 13 boys) also continued. In twenty years, female literacy rates have increased by only 5 per cent. Approximately one-fifth of the females and one-quarter of males had primary education, and only 9 per cent of females and 18 per cent of males had education beyond the primary level.[32] Despite evidence of continued gender differentials in human development indicators, the national government and donors did not come up with a policy and programming approach which used targets and incentives to lower maternal and child mortality rates or improve women's nutrition, though they did so to lower fertility rates. Only in the last few years have the donors become sensitive to the need to set targets and use incentives to close gender gaps in human development.

EMPOWERMENT

If progress in planning for achieving gender equality has been slow in the two countries, what about 'women's empowerment'? Are the women of Bangladesh and Tanzania being empowered? It is difficult to assess progress because women do not form a homogenous category. However, using the three criteria discussed earlier in Chapter 1 – strengthening the women's movement and participation in public action, and in national and local decisionmaking bodies – an impressionistic assessment of progress can be attempted.

Women's movement

The women's voice has certainly grown in strength, due largely to the increasing power of the women's movement in the last two decades. In Bangladesh, for example, in the early 1970s there were approximately a dozen women's organizations, which were primarily urban-based and involved in welfare-oriented work. The political parties and their mass fronts, such as students and trade unions, had separate women's wings, but they too were mostly active in urban areas. Mobilization of rural women was sporadic and generally took place around election time. By 1990, however, there had been several important changes. First, the number of women's organizations multiplied. According to one estimate, there were more than six hundred women's organizations registered with the Ministry of Social Welfare in 1985.[33] Second, many of the women's organizations shifted their orientation from welfare to development, enabling poor women to obtain access to credit, employment, income, literacy, health and family planning. Third, many of the non-government and women's organizations became active in rural areas, mobilizing rural women on a regular basis. While women fieldworkers and rural women's group meetings were oddities in the early 1970s, by 1990, according to one estimate, more than a million poor women were engaged in regular group meetings and activities, and over one hundred thousand women field workers were involved in projects to link poor women with development resources and services.[34] Finally, many of the women's organizations which did not have a grassroots base started establishing linkages with other organizations, especially NGOs, which focused on consciousness-raising and group organization and were active at the grassroots level. Through alliance-building women's groups were also able to raise gender issues in other forums.

Women's groups and organizations – Mahila Parishad, Ain Shalish Kendra Women for Women, Nari Pakkha, Ubinig, Nijera Kori, Saptogram, and so on – also started slowly to develop a women's agenda. With increasing frequency they began not only mobilizing women around issues which were traditionally regarded as women's issues, such as rape, dowry, violence, wife abuse, and trafficking in women; they also broadened the scope of the women's agenda to include many other developmental issues such as debt crisis, environmental crisis (e.g. dumping of toxic waste, salination and waterlogging), population-control policies and programmes, women's health issues and legal reforms. The close links forged between women researchers and activists facilitated the development of a women's voice and agenda.[35]

In Tanzania, UWT, the women's front of the ruling party, was for a long time the officially recognized women's voice. Women were also members of the mass organizations affiliated with the ruling party – the youth front (VIJANA), trade union (JUWATA), parents' organization (WAZAZI) and the cooperative union (WASHIRIKA). Women's autonomous organizations emerged in Tanzania only recently, as the government moved away from the single-party system. But the non-government women's groups are still largely urban-based advocacy groups with few rural links.

In Tanzania, too, the women's agenda has gradually changed. Initially focused on welfare issues, it expanded later to include many developmental issues, such as relieving women's work burden through the provision of water, fuel, grinding mills, and so on. In recent years, some of the NGOs, such as TAMWA, have raised the issues of rape, violence and sexual harassment. Another new group, BAWATA, has highlighted legal reforms to guarantee women's rights to own and inherit land and property. As in Bangladesh, in Tanzania women researchers have forged links with the activists and have played an important advocacy role.

Public action

Over the years, women's participation in public action has also increased in Bangladesh. Though women participated in the various political movements that led to the birth of Bangladesh they were never recognized as a political force. During the 1971 war of independence women played multiple roles, but they were primarily recognized in their role as victims. The raping by Pakistani soldiers of nearly two hundred thousand Bangladeshi women during the war, many of whom were later abandoned by their families to avoid dishonour to the family name, drew international and national attention. After independence, the government of Bangladesh accorded the rape victims the status of 'war heroines'. They were given privileges in public-sector education and employment similar to those accorded to the male freedom-fighters. But the shame associated with rape in a predominantly Muslim society prevented many women from publicly acknowledging their status as 'war heroines'.[36]

The war of independence was a watershed in raising women's consciousness about their subordination. The norm of female seclusion was shattered by the war, during which thousands of women could not be protected by their families against enemy aggression, and were later abandoned for no fault of their own. Their war experiences underscored the need for women to be self-reliant and autonomous. The proliferation of women's organizations, grassroots organizing and NGO development work in Bangladesh were in large measure due to the experiences of the liberation war. Women started taking part on their own as a group in public action; women's organizations became active in humanitarian crises like the flood of 1988, in social movements such as the opposition to fundamentalism, and in political struggles like the pro-democracy movement of 1990. Oikkya Baddha Nari Samaj, a united front of women's organizations, was in the forefront of the democracy movement in 1990: it was the Nari Samaj who first decided to break the curfew and challenge the government. Again, in the movement against the collaborators of the 1971 liberation war launched in 1992, women's groups played a major role. The movement known as Ghatak Dalal Nirmul Andolon (Eliminate Killers and Collaborators) was led by a woman, Jahanara Imam.

Women not only started to participate more actively in national political movements, they were also active in localized public actions. Women took a leading role in organizing protests against environmental degradation in a number of regions; they were also active in peasant movements for land rights. As the number of women wage-workers grew larger, they were increasingly drawn into trade-union activities, collective bargaining and movements to secure land and livelihood rights. Intermediary organizations played an important catalytic role in involving grassroots women in public action.

In the last decade, women's organizations have launched major campaigns for the enactment of new and stringent laws providing deterrent punishment for violence against women; the enactment of a uniform family code for all religious communities; full ratification of UNCEDAW, and implementation of labour laws including ILO conventions. Women's groups and organizations also started using alternative media and forms of communication such as street theatre, role-play, posters, videos and so on, to raise mass awareness about gender issues.

Decisionmaking

Women's participation in public decisionmaking bodies has also increased in the last two decades, though most of this 'progress' is due to the women's quota. In Bangladesh, the female quota in national parliament was raised from 5 per cent of seats in 1972 to 10 per cent of seats in 1979. Similarly, from 1977 onwards two nominated women members were added to the local government bodies. The quota system was criticized by many feminists on the grounds that it depended on indirect election, giving the predominantly male members of the majority party an opportunity to select women from their own party. Women parliamentarians from the reserved seats were essentially handpicked to support the party in power. The system of nomination and indirect election also removed these women from the rough and tumble of electoral politics and nurturing of a political constituency.

Women's groups demanded an alternative form of female quota – either reserved seats which women could contest directly, or a quota within parties which would require parties to nominate a certain

percentage of women candidates.[37] But successive governments continued with the system of indirect election for reserved women's seats
in parliament and local bodies. The number of women directly elected
to the national parliament increased slowly. While there were no directly
elected women in the 1972 parliament, 5 women were directly elected
(out of 300 seats) in the 1991 parliamentary election. The leaders of
both the government and the major opposition party also happened to
be women: though they inherited their leadership positions after the
assassination of their male kin (husband and father) and had not worked
up through the party ranks, both Khaleda Zia and Hasina Wazed
managed to continue as party leaders for over a decade. In the
opposition political party, the Awami League, two other women, Sajeda
Chowdhury and Motia Chowdhury, are in the top ranks of party
leadership.

As in Bangladesh, in Tanzania women's representation in the national
parliament and other local-level bodies was ensured through women's
reserved seats. Women won direct elections to only two seats in the
mainland and one seat in Zanzibar. But UWT had twenty-five reserved
seats, and the two front organizations, WAZAZI and VIJANA, had
one woman each from their reserved quota of four and two seats
respectively.[38] In regional and district committees and in village-level
organizations women's representation was also low. According to one
survey conducted in 1980, only 6.5 per cent of all village managers
were women. Women's representation in central party organization was
also low: only 11 per cent of national executive council members and
5.6 per cent of central committee members were women; similarly only
8 per cent of leadership positions in JUWATA were held by women.[39]

The donors' role

What has been the donors' role in strengthening aid-recipient women's
voices and defining their own agenda in the partner countries? The
donors have played a double-edged role. On the one hand, they have
had a positive role in funding autonomous women's organizations,
research on women, and grassroots NGO work. In Bangladesh, for
example, the activities of the majority of well-known women's organizations were funded by donors. Only a few organizations like Mahila
Parishad did not solicit external donor funding and were successful in
raising local funds. Research on women and gender issues was also
largely donor-funded, and data-collection and gender-disaggregation of
statistics undertaken mostly at donors' insistence. Grassroots development work, whether by government agencies or by NGOs, was primarily
underwritten by the donors. Up to now donors have kept a relative

distance from the political parties and parliament, but recently there has been discussion of donor assistance for training of parliamentarians and local government representatives. With emerging concerns about democracy and human rights it is expected that donors will start funding activities in areas directly related to political mobilization and participation. In Tanzania, too, research on women, grassroots development work and autonomous women's organizations have been heavily dependent on donor assistance.

On the negative side, donor funding often made the women's organizations and NGOs donor-driven. Instead of developing their own voice, in many cases they were coopted to sell the donors' agenda. The pressure of satisfying donor-established performance criteria often kept these organizations too focused on the donors rather than on their own domestic constituencies. In the last two decades very little progress has been achieved in changing the donors' funding policies from project- to process-oriented aid, a change that would give the women's organizations and NGOs greater autonomy and time to develop their own voice. The governments' policies were also not supportive of strengthening the voice of autonomous women's groups.

In both Bangladesh and Tanzania, women's groups and organizations have started taking some tentative steps towards defining their own agendas. Though fragmented and issue-based, women's groups have through a variety of strategies including lobbying, advocacy, agitation and media publicity begun to influence public opinion and public policy discourses. But they have not yet been able to form strong common-cause coalitions around women's issues. In Bangladesh, for example, in 1985, violence was for a time a rallying point for all women's organizations, but soon the unity of ranks broke down and different groups adopted different strategies to combat violence. Similarly, despite common concerns about the rise of fundamentalism, women's organizations could not decide upon a common strategy. Women's groups were successful in lobbying political parties to put forward gender issues in the party platforms, but they were unable to put enough pressure on parties to take these issues forward and translate them into policies and actions. Indeed, women's groups are still a fair way off from articulating a clear feminist vision of social transformation. A few groups have started talking about an alternative vision of development, but this vision has not been disseminated even among the majority of women's groups, let alone the wider body of citizens. A major challenge for the future is to define the feminist vision of development much more clearly and bring that vision into play in mainstream development discourse.

SUMMARY

Measuring progress is difficult, because donors and their development partners have not established any indicators to monitor the achievement of their goals. The donors generally monitored adoption of various procedures and implementation of different activities, but these could not be directly linked to development impacts on the ground. They generally generated two types of quantitative data, women's share of staff and budget, which measured progress in mainstreaming women in agency resources. Available data indicate slow progress in increasing women's share of agency personnel and in increasing WID assistance.

A review of agency documents also shows slow progress in mainstreaming gender issues in agency discourses. There was progress in identification of gender issues in a wide variety of economic sectors. In social sectors, progress was achieved in redefining issues from a gender perspective. Macro-policy discourses also started to become gender-aware. But the agencies were far more successful in discussing the issues and coopting the language of change than they were in actually changing policies and programmes and reallocating resources to bring about changes on the ground. The major barriers to achieving gender equality – the gender gap in reproductive labour, unequal entitlement to productive resources, and women's lack of voice in decisionmaking – were well articulated in agency discourses, but no serious attempt was made to investigate the policy options and budgetary costs necessary to tackle these gender-specific constraints.

In the two partner countries, slow progress was achieved in improving women's education and health. Women's need to earn cash income grew faster than employment opportunities, and a large number of women were pushed into insecure casual jobs and self-employment. Gender gaps in education, health, employment, income and decisionmaking continued. But donors and governments were slow to use targets and incentives as planning tools to promote gender equality.

In the last two decades, there has also been gradual progress in women defining their own and the national agenda. Research and public debate on gender issues has increased. The number of women's organizations and groups has multiplied, and women's groups have started to take an autonomous stand on a wide variety of national issues. But these groups still remain fragmented, unable to articulate a clearly defined development agenda and forge alliances with a wider network of citizens' groups to mobilize large-scale popular support behind their vision of alternative development.

NOTES

1. Teresa Hayter, *Aid as Imperialism*, Penguin, Harmondsworth 1971; Eirik G. Jensen, 'Interest Groups and Development Assistance: The Case of Bangladesh', in *SQKJELYSPAU HJELPA*, 1992.

2. Personal interview, 1991.

3. United Nations, *The Nairobi Forward-Looking Strategies for the Advancement of Women*, 1986.

4. Ron Grosz, quoted in Aruna Rao et al., eds., *Gender Training and Development Planning: Learning from Experience*, Population Council and Christian Michelsten Institute, 1992, p. 42.

5. UNDP, 'A Review of 1989 WID Questionnaire', mimeo, 1989.

6. The World Bank, *Excellence through Equality: An Increased Role for Women in the World Bank*, Report of the Advisory Group on Higher Level Women's Issues, April 1992.

7. The World Bank Staff Association, *Report on Status of Higher Level Women in the World Bank Group*, November 1989, p. 11.

8. Ibid.

9. *Equal Times*, United Nations, 1987.

10. UNDP, *Women in Development: Report of the Administrator*, 30 April 1990.

11. The World Bank, *Women in Development: A Progress Report of the World Bank Initiative*, 1989, p. 24.

12. Ibid., p. 27.

13. Ibid., p. 31.

14. UNDP, *Women in Development*.

15. United Nations, *1989 World Survey on the Role of Women in Development*; Susan Joekes, *Women in the World Economy*, Oxford University Press, New York 1987; FAO, *Second Progress Report on WCAARRD Programme of Action Including the Role of Women in Rural Development*, Rome 1987; Noeleen Heyzer, ed., *Women Farmers in Rural Change in Asia*, APDC, Kuala Lumpur 1987.

16. United Nations, *1989 World Survey on the Role of Women in Development*; Swasti Mitter, *Common Fate, Common Bond*, Pluto Press, London 1987; Guy Standing, 'Global Feminization through Flexible Labor', *World Development*, July 1989, pp. 1077–96; Noeleen Heyzer, ed., *Daughters in Industry*, APDC, Kuala Lumpur 1988.

17. United Nations, *1989 World Survey on the Role of Women in Development*; Report of the World Conference to Review and Appraise the Achievement of the United Nations Decade for Women: Equality, Development and Peace, Nairobi, 15–26 July 1985.

18. OECD/DAC, Aid Review, *Memorandum of Norway*, Paris, 1989.

19. OECD/DAC, Aid Review, *Memorandum of Norway*, Paris, 1990.

20. OECD/DAC, Aid Review, *Memorandum of Canada*, Paris, 1988/89.

21. The World Bank, *The World Development Report: Environment and Development*, 1992.

22. Commonwealth Secretariat, *Engendering Adjustment in the 1990s*, Report of the Commonwealth Expert Group on Women and Structural Adjustment, 1990.

23. CIRDAP, *Monitoring Adjustment and Poverty*, Dhaka 1993, quoted in UNDP, *Empowerment of Women*, 1994 Report on Human Development in Bangladesh, p. 6.

24. United Nations, *World's Women: 1970–1990*, New York 1991.

25. Ibid.

26. Ibid.

27. Rounaq Jahan, *Women and Development in Bangladesh: Challenges and Opportunities*, The Ford Foundation, Dhaka 1989, p. 13.

28. Ibid., p. 13.

29. Ibid., p. 8.

30. Ibid., p. 9.

31. Ibid., p. 9.

32. Ibid., p. 8.

33. Roushan Jahan, 'Women's Movement in Bangladesh: Concerns and Challenges', in *Alternatives*, vol. II, DAWN 1991. p. 231.

34. Janice Jiggins, unpublished consultancy report, The World Bank, 1987.

35. Roushan Jahan, 'Women's Movement in Bangladesh', p. 242.

36. Rounaq Jahan, *Women in Bangladesh*, Ford Foundation, Dhaka 1973.

37. *Women in Development*, Report of the Task Force on Bangladesh, Strategies for the 1990s, Dhaka UPL, pp. 349–51.

38. NORAD, *Action Plan for Women in Development: Tanzania*, mimeo, pp. 13–15.

39. Ibid.

CHAPTER 6

FUTURE CHALLENGES

> Behind the blaring headlines of the world's many conflicts and emergencies, there lies a silent crisis.... This is not a crisis that will respond to emergency relief. Or to fitful policy interventions. It requires a long, quiet process of sustainable human development ... [a] development that not only generates economic growth but distributes its benefits equitably, that regenerates the environment rather than destroying it; that empowers people rather than marginalizing them. It is development that gives priority to the poor, enlarging their choices and opportunities and providing for their participation in decisions that affect their lives. It is development that is pro-people, pro-nature, pro-jobs and pro-women.
>
> UNDP, *Human Development Report 1994*, p. iii

A report in 1975 by the International Labour Organization (ILO) caught world attention by pointing out that while 'women and girls constitute one-half of the world's population and one-third of the official labour force' and 'perform nearly two-thirds of work hours', they 'receive only one-tenth of the world's income and less than one-hundredth of the world's property'.[1]

Nearly twenty years later, a report by the United Nations – UNDP's *Human Development Report 1994* – found that, despite advances in labour-force participation, education and health, women still constitute about two-thirds of the world's illiterates, hold fewer than half of the jobs on the market and are paid half as much as men for work of equal value. Women make up only about 10 per cent of the world's parliamentarians and less than 4 per cent of cabinet members. The report concludes that 'in no society are women secure or treated equally'.[2]

The unmistakable achievements in areas like education and health show that progress is possible, but the continued disparities in others such as income and decisionmaking indicate that there is still a long way to go. The contrasting patterns of progress for women mirror the contrasts we find in the overall achievements in human development. While the global GDP has risen sevenfold in the last fifty years and the share of world population enjoying a 'fairly satisfactory human development level' has increased from 25 per cent to 60 per cent over the last three decades, the disparity between the richest 20 per cent and the poorest 20 per cent of the world's population doubled during the same period, and one-quarter of humanity is still unable to meet its basic human needs. The few rich nations of the world still consume four-fifths of natural capital.[3]

There is a growing realization that ultimately the persistent inequalities do not serve anybody's interest; in fact, they often have the boomerang effect, that the 'development patterns that perpetuate today's inequalities are neither sustainable nor worth sustaining'.[5] But this realization is still abstract. The world community has yet to commit itself to a clear blueprint for creating a more just and equal world for the twenty-first century. There is a growing ferment; the world is restructuring itself; people are demanding a greater voice in decisions affecting their lives and choices. Old priorities, policies and institutions are being challenged, but the shapes of new policies and institutions are far from clear.

At a time of restructuring it is essential to assess past policies and actions and to define future strategies. This study was undertaken in that spirit. Policies and measures to promote gender equality and women's advancement are reviewed in different development contexts – in the bilateral and multilateral donor agencies and in the two aid-recipient countries – to illuminate our understanding of achievements, gaps, constraints and future priorities.

ACHIEVEMENTS

The statistical evidence about continued disparities should not detract us from recognizing the major achievements of the last two decades. There has been a sea-change in knowledge and awareness. Affirmative-action policies have been introduced. Special measures have been designed to remove barriers to women's participation. Women's voices are stronger than ever. And women are increasingly learning to take control of their own lives and bring their perspective to bear on decisions affecting their communities, nations and the planet. These changes in awareness, expertise, policies, laws and women's voice were brought about by the efforts of many different actors – women's movements, as well as national governments and international donor organizations.

Awareness

The most significant achievement has been in levels of awareness. Awareness has improved on many fronts, and perceptions about women have changed. Consciousness has been raised: first of all of women themselves, but also of mainstream institutions, who can no longer afford to dismiss gender issues as irrelevant or insignificant. The awareness of officials serving national governments and international agencies has increased. There is a growing sense of public accountability. Government and donor agency documents reflect these changes in awareness. Most notably:

- Women are no longer portrayed simply as beneficiaries of social policies and programmes: their significant economic contributions as wage and non-wage workers, as families' sole and primary breadwinners and as labourers in export-oriented sectors are now well recognized.

- Women's rights and abilities to make choices and take control of their lives are increasingly being accepted: their victim image is being discarded.

- Women are no longer projected as part of the problem but as part of the solution. Their knowledge and perspective in attaining the objectives of sustainable development is gaining recognition.

- Discriminatory practices which used to be regarded either as natural or in the private domain, like sexual harassment and domestic violence, have attained public policy attention.

Expertise

Expertise on gender issues has also grown significantly, due in large measure to donor efforts. In many ways WID was a trailblazer in donor agencies, the first crosscutting mandate, which was followed by mandates on the environment, human rights, good governance and other emerging issues. The act of mainstreaming women's concerns has pioneered many institutional and operational strategies which have served as models for other mandates. Expertise was developed by combining research and action. Over the years, demands for WID/GAD experts increased in donor agencies and national governments, as gender expertise and a gender perspective were brought to bear on policies and programmes in various sectors, such as agriculture, micro-enterprises, and health and population. The growth of expertise is particularly demonstrated by:

- development of different analytical methodologies for research and data collection;
- designing of various procedures and tools for planning and operations; and
- development of different training methodologies and modules.

Affirmative action policies

A variety of affirmative action measures were designed and implemented which improved women's participation in decisionmaking bodies and increased their access to development opportunities. These included:

- quotas and targets in personnel policies;
- quotas in representative institutions; and
- quotas in the various development programmes – training, scholarship, credit, and so on.

Measures removing discrimination

Progress has been made in adopting measures to remove discriminatory barriers against women's equality. WID/GAD policy objectives heightened the importance of identifying obstacles to women's participation and designing measures to overcome them. Specific measures adopted by countries included:

- legal reforms to give women equal rights in personal, civic and political affairs;
- laws to combat violence against women; and
- access to institutions and jobs hitherto barred to women.

Women's voices

WID/GAD policies and measures stressed the importance of consultation with women so that their perspective could inform policy, programme and project decisions. Donors have funded women's organizations and women's participation in meetings and conferences. Women's voices are increasingly being heard in local, national and international fora, and they have emerged as champions not simply of women's causes but of a wide range of issues such as the environment, human rights, democracy, people's participation, and so on. Though women's participation in mainstream political institutions has not increased significantly, their numbers in national and international bureaucracies have steadily grown, in part due to affirmative-action policies. The unmistakable strength of the women's voice is evidenced by:

- women's increasing participation in different people's movements and organizations;
- women's leadership of non-government organizations and of various struggles for the rights of marginalized groups; and

- women's initiatives to direct world attention to peace and democracy, and to a people-centred concept of development.

FUTURE PRIORITIES

The achievements of the past decades have been hard won. Twenty years ago, when the women's movement raised the issue of gender equality, national governments and international donor agencies accepted the goal in principle, but they did not have any ready-made policy or instrument to address the set of concerns brought forward by women. Developing policies, designing tools and implementing them took time. The goal of the women's movement was nothing short of changing the very direction of development. Removing gender disparities in human development and access to opportunities implied changing priorities and redistributing resources; the elimination of discriminatory practices meant changing laws and customs that have prevailed over centuries. There was resistance to change, created by ignorance, bias and conflicts of interest. The women's agenda was not clearly understood or appreciated, and it was also threatening as it implied fundamental restructuring of society. Even when awareness was raised and WID policies and measures were adopted, implementation was difficult.

There is a growing realization that, though a good start has been made, many of the objectives laid down by the donors and their development partners have still not been achieved. Gaps have emerged between intentions and results. Policy objectives were not clear and needed specificity. There have been few measurable goals against which progress can be measured. Policy and programme interventions have not been adequate to ensure results. Institutional frameworks have been weak and required strengthening. The experiences of the last two decades indicate a number of future priorities (see Figure 6.1).

Specify objectives

As discussed in Chapter 2, policy objectives were articulated in a broad and diffuse manner. Process-focused objectives like 'integration' and 'mainstreaming' were highlighted, which distracted attention from the substantive objectives of gender equality, women's empowerment, women's advancement, and so on. The distinction between ends (e.g. gender equality) and means (e.g. mainstreaming) were not clarified. In donor agencies, concerns over means often took precedence over ends. As a result, donors spent a lot of effort in devising instruments and tracking the progress of WID institutionalization in agency processes

Figure 6.1 Future Priorities

1. Objectives
   - Clarify objectives
   - Establish measurable goals and timetables

2. Financial Plan
   - Prepare cost estimates
   - Identify sources of financing
   - Plan innovative ways of raising additional resources

3. Policy, Planning and Programming
   - Improve policy analysis
   - Improve statistics and database
   - Engender policy dialogue
   - Bring gender perspective into programme development early on

4. Institutional Framework
   - Strengthen internal accountability
   - Improve public accountability
   - Establish monitoring indicators and mechanisms
   - Rationalize resources and functions of special machineries

5. Development Partnership
   - Strengthen institutional capacity of aid-recipients
   - Strengthen partnership processes
   - Build aid recipients' abilities to set their own agendas

6. Political Will
   - Strengthen women's networks and movements
   - Improve lobbying capacity
   - Encourage participation in civic and political bodies
   - Increase male support
   - Strengthen North–South dialogue

and procedures. And indeed they attained a fair amount of success in legitimizing and institutionalizing WID/GAD. But the donors were far less successful in designing policy- and programme-level innovations and monitoring progress in attaining their substantive objectives.

In addition to blurring the distinction between ends and means, policy statements often did not distinguish between long-term and short-term objectives, and priorities were rarely established. The relationship between WID/GAD policy objectives and the agency and governments' overall objectives was not clear. Indeed, in many cases, the overall priorities and mode of operation ran counter to the attainment of the substantive goals of WID/GAD.

The policy statements of only a few donors referred specifically to the core concerns of the women's movement. On the whole, agencies and governments did not specify how their policies addressed the women's agenda. More specifically they avoided the issue of the need for a fundamental restructuring of development paradigms.

Donors and their partners have generally neglected to establish specific targets and timetables to achieve their goals, though in areas where measurable goals, targets and timetables were established – like personnel policy, scholarship and training, population and family planning programmes – progress could be monitored and results were achieved. Some donors established budgetary targets, which again were met. NORAD achieved its target of 30 per cent of its agricultural-sector assistance reaching women by 1991; the Netherlands have set a target of 50 per cent of development assistance meeting OECD/DAC/WID's statistical criteria by 1998.

In future, articulation of policy objectives needs to be more specific. They should:

• Clarify policy objectives. Instrumental (e.g. mainstreaming) and substantive (e.g. gender equality, women's advancement and women's empowerment) objectives should be differentiated. The distinction should be made between long-term and short-term objectives. WID/GAD policy objectives should be linked with the agencies' and governments' overall policy objectives. An agenda-setting approach to mainstreaming should be emphasized. Women's vision of development and not simply women's development should be highlighted.

• Establish measurable goals and timetables. Measurable goals and timetables should be established to achieve progress in substantive objectives such as gender equality and women's empowerment.

Targets and timetables are needed particularly in the following three critical areas:

Human development For the next decade, targets should be established to eliminate women's illiteracy, increase their school enrolment rates and participation in science and technical training, especially in new and emerging technologies. Targets should also be established to eliminate severe malnutrition, reduce maternal and child mortality rates and improve access to primary and reproductive health care. UNDP's *Human Development Report 1994*, for example, has proposed a set of basic human development targets for the period 1995–2005. These include universal access to basic education, primary healthcare, child immunization and safe drinking water; elimination of severe malnutrition and the gender gap in literacy; reduction by half of adult illiteracy, maternal and child mortality and malnutrition rates; and provisioning of a basic family planning package to all willing adult couples.[6]

Decisionmaking   Targets should be established to improve over the next ten years women's participation in decisionmaking bodies at international, regional, national and local levels. International agencies and national governments have already established quotas and targets: their implementation should be strictly monitored and new targets established to achieve parity in decisionmaking.

Poverty alleviation   Targets should be established to reduce women's poverty by half during the next decade. Proactive measures and budget earmarks should be used to improve women's access to credit, employment and social services.

Prepare a financial plan

A major weakness of past WID/GAD policies and measures was the absence of a realistic financial plan to achieve the objectives; costing was also not considered essential as the objectives were articulated in a process-focused manner. It was assumed that with greater integration and mainstreaming women will increasingly obtain access to regular budget resources. As the special machineries were envisioned to perform a catalytic function only, they were allocated a small separate budget for innovative and promotional work. Operational departments were mandated to address gender issues in their programmes, but they did not establish any clear rationale of resource allocation for WID/GAD actions: planning, programming and budget allocation for WID/GAD were generally made ad hoc.

In future, priority attention should be paid to the following:

- Preparing cost estimates for achieving gender-equality targets. Cost estimates to achieve targets have been prepared in other programme areas, such as the environment, population and human development.

For example, UNDP's *Human Development Report 1994* estimates an annual cost of US$30 to 40 billion for the achievement of essential human development targets.[7]

• Identifying the sources of possible finance: what proportion can be generated from redirecting budget priorities – for example, from military expenditure to social development – and what proportion would require additional revenue.

• Planning innovative ways of raising additional resources. Again, *Human Development Report 1994* has suggested several new sources, such as a pollution tax or taxing global foreign exchange movement.[8] Other national and international sources need to be explored to finance the targets of gender equality.

Improve policy analysis, planning and programming

Progress has been achieved over the last two decades in undertaking policy analysis, and in designing analytical methodologies, planning and programming instruments. Development of operational tools took time and often lagged behind changes in agency priorities. The first decade was spent in gathering evidence from research and field projects, and designing tools to address gender issues in the context of projects. In the second decade, efforts were launched to undertake policy analysis from a gender perspective and develop new operational tools as agencies started emphasizing policy- and programme-level interventions. The gender-differentiated impact of structural adjustment programmes (SAPs) was documented and special programme components were designed to buffer SAPs' adverse impact on women.

However, gendered policy analysis and programme development has only recently started. In only a few sectors – such as health and population, agriculture and micro-enterprises – have policies and programmes been analysed from a gender perspective. Gender issues still remain unexplored in a wide range of macro- and sectoral policies and programmes. Development of policies and programmes to address women's core agenda – such as poverty reduction and equality in human development, decisionmaking and entitlement – similarly lags behind, constraining consideration of gender issues in policy dialogues.

The policies and practices of transnational companies (TNCs) is another grey area. Their influence in shaping the global economy and in exploiting women as cheap labour in export-oriented industries is well recognized. But it is hard to devise measures to change these policies, as TNCs remain largely above public scrutiny and are not accountable to national governments.

A women's vision of alternative development also remains un-developed, and no path has yet been mapped out as to how this could come about, especially what cost-shifting would be required to bring about a transformed agenda. Limitation of knowledge and absence of instruments are not the only problems. Even in situations where infor-mation exists and tools are available, legitimizing them can be a challenge. Traditional planners, who are used to quantitative cost–benefit analysis, a top-down approach and universally applicable technical fixes, find WID/GAD analytical tools difficult to fit into their daily operations, as these tools emphasize qualitative indicators such as empowerment and grassroots organizing, and a bottom-up approach of consultation with the 'target' population.

In future greater attention needs to be paid to link macro- and micro-perspectives in order to illuminate gender issues in the following critical areas:

Policy analysis Macro-policies currently influencing global economic changes – such as trade, science and technology, and information and communication – should be investigated from a gender perspective. Policy instruments need to be developed to facilitate the achievement of women's core agenda.

Statistics and database The lack of gender-disaggregated statistics and data is still a major obstacle to raising awareness and understanding, undertaking policy analysis, designing gender-responsive programmes, and monitoring and evaluation. Agencies' and governments' capacity to collect, analyse and use gender-disaggregated statistics and data should be improved.

Programme development A gender perspective should be built from the beginning in the new and emerging programme areas such as good governance and participatory development, human rights and sustainable development.

Policy dialogue Women's participation as decisionmakers should be ensured and debates on macroeconomic and sectoral policies should reflect a gendered perspective.

Strengthen the institutional framework

The institutional framework designed for the implementation of WID/ GAD policies had certain limitations, which were explored in Chapter 3.

First, the policies dictated agency-wide responsibility for implementation of WID mandates, but they did not institute accountability measures to ensure agency compliance. Generally, compliance was greater in agencies that worked under strong public scrutiny. Second, WID/GAD measures were introduced but their systematic use was not tracked; more important, key indicators were not developed to assess the effects on the aid recipients. Third, the mandates and resources of the special machineries, the linchpin of the institutional framework, did not match.

The machineries were given the near-impossible task of criticizing and reforming the very organizations they serve, mainly through catalytic and promotional work. There was no consensus about what was expected from the special machineries and how they should go about performing their catalytic role, and they faced contrasting demands from their two constituencies, on the inside (the agency) and outside (the women's movement). Satisfying both was difficult, as their perceptions of 'good WID performance' differed. To succeed inside, the machineries needed to fit into the organizational mould and play by the rules; to succeed outside they needed to challenge the organization and change the rules. The dual pressure led the machineries to take on multiple functions – policy and strategy development, technical support to operational departments, a watchdog function over the organization, and networking with outside women's organizations. But the staff and budgetary resources were not adequate to perform the variety of tasks the machineries undertook. Additionally, the staffing pattern was weak, the machineries were frequently moved around in the organization, and leadership positions were often kept vacant, which created a sense of insecurity among staff.

Yet in most organizations, solutions to the structural problems of the machineries were sought in individual personalities: individuals holding WID/GAD positions were either acclaimed or blamed for their personal traits rather than their professional qualities. In the early years of the Decade, agencies recruited feminists from outside to fill WID positions, but later the agencies turned to 'managers', as it was believed that feminists were confrontational and pushed their male colleagues too hard! Thus personal image became an important consideration for holding WID/GAD positions. The former director of the WID programme at UNDP, for example, went on record to say that the fact that all WID staff were 'married mothers' looked reassuring to colleagues.[9] Additionally, since WID offices were heavily dependant on extra budgetary resources, in many multilateral agencies these positions were regarded as 'donors' jobs' – that is, women from donor countries were recruited to fill WID positions. Only recently has there been a shift away from donor country candidates for these jobs.

In future, institutional frameworks need to be strengthened, especially in the following areas:

Internal accountability Measures should be established to hold organizations accountable for WID mandates. Several steps would facilitate internal accountability: measurable targets to evaluate performance, holding key programmes managers accountable through performance appraisal, and strengthening women's voices in various checkpoints within agencies such as steering committees, programme teams and project approval boards.

Public accountability Unrestricted disclosure of data and documents and creation of advisory bodies with representation from the civil society would foster public accountability. Similarly, accountability to the aid recipients should be established through the setting up of joint commissions, for example.

Monitoring Key quantitative and qualitative indicators should be identified to assess results of WID/GAD measures, and monitoring mechanisms should be established to track progress on the key indicators.

Special machineries Resources and functions of special machineries should be rationalized: staff and budgetary resources should be commensurate with functions, and the staffing pattern comparable with other offices in the organizations. The catalytic role of WID/GAD staff and the implementation role of programme managers should be well defined. Professional qualifications rather than personal attributes for holding WID/GAD positions should be emphasized. Staff should be given institutional security and recognition for good performance.

Build development partnerships

The need to build development partnerships was clear to WID/GAD advocates from the beginning. As the primary process of changing gender roles and relations was perceived to take place in the cultural domain, donors were particularly careful to stress the importance of country-specific contexts and aid recipients' own initiatives. NGOs and women's organizations were recognized as critical partners in promoting the mission.

But despite the greater commitment to build partnerships, changing the established pattern of donor–recipient relationships proved difficult. The disparities in perspectives, priorities and institutional capacities hampered the development of partnerships. Whereas donors emphasized the objective of 'integration', prioritizing the development of policies, processes, procedures and tools to change their own practices, aid recipients prioritized changes in the condition of women through mobilization, and innovative experimentation on the ground.

The institutional capacities of donors and aid recipients also differed. Donor agencies designed WID/GAD policies, guidelines, analytical and operational tools, and training methodologies. Expertise on gender issues developed in mainstream research and training institutions, and within NGOs in donor countries. The networking between women's organizations and the WID/GAD offices in the donor agencies worked in a mutually supportive way. In the partner countries, by contrast, national machineries did not prioritize policy and institutional development, and gender expertise developed not in mainstream research and training institutions but in NGOs and autonomous women's organizations, or simply among freelance consultants.

As WID/GAD became institutionalized, gaps emerged between the working practices of donors and aid recipients, due largely to differences in institutional capacities. NGOs and women's organizations in the aid-recipient countries developed alternative concepts and methodologies grounded on their grassroots experiences (such as empowerment and participatory development), challenging established models and methods; but they generally lacked the time and institutional capacity to package and export their concepts and models. This task was left largely in the hands of donor-country institutions. Many of the WID/GAD methodologies developed as a result of North–South cross-fertilization, but the division of labour and disparities in institutional capacities resulted in Northern institutions controlling the end products.

The institutionalization of WID also resulted in a demand for WID/GAD experts. Again, technical assistance provided by donor-country experts became a debated issue as their expertise was challenged by the aid recipients. In many instances, donors recruited nationals as consultants and WID focal points. But this attempt to utilize and bolster national expertise sometimes resulted in using the nationals' experience to serve donors' priorities rather than assisting aid recipients to set their own agendas. Donors rarely pursued a systematic strategy to build gender competence in the mainstream national institutions of the aid-recipient countries, such as central and local government, universities, research and training institutions, NGOs and women's organizations.

In future, greater attention needs to be paid to:

• Strengthening the institutional capacity of the aid recipients. Capacity-building efforts should not be limited to national machineries. Gender expertise should be built into all mainstream national institutions,

especially in sectoral ministries of government, statistical and planning offices, universities and research and training institutions.

- Strengthening partnership processes. Structures should be developed
for regular consultation and dialogue between the various development partners, such as governments, NGOs, the private sector and
donors. Dialogues should clarify the roles and responsibilities of different partners and facilitate the building of common ground.

- Building aid recipients' abilities to set their own agendas. The partner
governments should be helped to develop their own national gender-
equity policies, based on extensive consultation with NGOs and wom-
en's organizations, and to design institutional mechanisms, including
accountability and monitoring measures, to implement these policies.

Sustain a political will

Gender equality appeared on the global development agenda because of
the international women's movement, and in the final analysis it is the
political pressure of the movement that continues to keep women on
the agenda. Individual women within governments and outside them
are in relatively weak positions in all countries, but together the women's
networks and movement have emerged as a force to be reckoned with.
They have learnt to lobby and mobilize for their cause and forge alliances with other people's movements, and they have increasingly gained
understanding and support from men. Women working for national and
international bureaucracies have also been successful in operating within
them, overcoming bureaucratic blockages through alliance-building with
colleagues and gaining the support of their bosses.

But the future presents many challenges. The role of the proactive
state is being threatened by the ascendance of the market, and social
policies are under attack. The donor agencies are faced with multiple
mandates. Numerous people's movements have emerged. The women's
movement itself is not monolithic: the differences within the movement
between North and South, young and old, moderates and radicals have
to be continuously negotiated. The growing strength of fundamentalism
in many parts of the world poses a threat to the movement. Male
support and responsibility is still weak. The strong inside–outside link
forged early in the Decade for Women has weakened, as with greater
institutionalization women within bureaucracies have turned inward
towards their own organization for support rather than outward to
women's groups and the women's movement.

However, the achievement of the women's agenda would require the sustained commitment of all development partners. To keep political will alive efforts are required to:

- Strengthen women's networks and movements nationally, regionally and internationally. The mass base of support of the women's movement is narrow: in many countries, detractors accuse feminists of being representatives of a small elite. The movement needs to broaden its constituency and support by championing the interests of working-class women.

- Improve the lobbying capacity of women's groups. Women's organizations have traditionally been strong in grassroots organizing and delivery of services, and have only recently started to lobby for policy reform. This capacity to lobby and dialogue with policymakers needs to be strengthened.

- Encourage women's participation in civic and political bodies. Women's participation in mainstream civic and political organizations is still peripheral, which explains the continued marginalization of WID/GAD issues in policy dialogues. Affirmative-action policies need to be undertaken to increase women's participation.

- Increase male support. Gender issues are still largely perceived as a women's cause, rather than the cause of both women and men. Greater awareness needs to be encouraged concerning the interests of both men and women in promoting gender equality.

- Strengthen North–South dialogue. North–South solidarity has played a critical role in keeping women on the agenda. This solidarity needs to be continuously renewed through dialogues in which differences in priorities and perspectives can be debated and common ground negotiated.

NOTES

1. ILO, *Women at Work*, Geneva, January 1975, quoted in United Nations, *The State of the World's Women*, 1979.

2. UNDP, *Human Development Report 1994*, p. 31.

3. Ibid., pp. 1–2.

4. Susan George, *The Debt Boomerang: How Third World Debt Harms All*, Westview Press, Boulder 1992.

5. UNDP, *Human Development Report 1994*, p. 19.

6. Ibid., p. 7.

7. Ibid., p. 7.

8. Ibid., p. 9.

9. Hilkka Pietila and Ingrid Edie, *The Role of the Nordic Countries in the Advancement of Women within the United Nations System*, Report no. 16, UNDP 1990, p. 43.

CHAPTER 7

CONCLUSION

THE ELUSIVE AGENDA

This study has reviewed the policies and measures undertaken over the last two decades in different development contexts to promote gender equality and women's advancement, and has attempted to draw a balance-sheet of achievements and shortfalls. Despite significant gains in a number of fronts – such as in knowledge and awareness; in the introduction of mandates and special measures; and in strengthening the voice of women – the fundamental objectives of the Southern women's movement, transforming social and gender relations and creating a just and equal world, still elude us. The vision of that movement quoted at the beginning of this study, articulated so well by DAWN, remains a distant goal. And indeed, poverty among women has increased even in the richest countries; women's labour-force participation has grown, but the terms and conditions of their employment have not improved. The central issue explored by the study is: why has progress been so elusive for women? What explains the contradictory trends – heightened advocacy and awareness of gender issues on the one hand, and the growing poverty of the world's women on the other?

The study addresses some crucial questions: is progress elusive because the women's agenda has not been clearly defined, or is it because policies and measures have not adequately addressed that agenda? How should progress be measured: by efforts or by results? Are policies and strategies essentially on the right track, needing only more time and better implementation, or do they need reorientation?

There are, of course, no simple answers to the above questions. The women's movement did articulate an agenda – equality, empowerment, and the transformation of existing development paradigms emerged as core concerns. But this challenged mainstream thinking and the global power structure so dramatically that the initial response of international and national bureaucracies was to ignore a large part of the women's agenda, on the ground that these social issues did not 'fit' into agency operations. Their stand was countered by the advocates of gender equality in two ways. At one level, efforts were made to demonstrate why agencies and governments should be concerned about gender issues, and how they can be 'fitted' into agency processes, procedures and operations.[1] The efficiency and anti-poverty arguments were developed to justify investment in women, arguing that such investment would lead to economic growth as well as poverty alleviation.[2] At another level, the women's movement pressed for changing the existing assumptions, theories and models of development. It underscored the importance of social policies and the need for a people-centred development model. The movement urged changing organizational rules and cultures to move towards inclusive and participatory processes, women's voices in decisionmaking, greater transparency and accountability, and so on.

Agency and state policies responded more favourably to the first level of argument, which did not demand structural changes. But in areas where investment in women required the redistribution of power and resources – sharing responsibilities in reproductive labour, gender equality in land and property rights, a voice in decisionmaking, and so on – agencies and states were less responsive. The idea of investment in women could be sold to the agencies when it was possible to demonstrate that there would be quick economic returns (e.g. income and employment projects, micro-enterprises, export-led growth strategies), or if it was linked to reaching other development goals (e.g. controlling population growth), but the proposition was less successful if it was made on the grounds of women's rights, or the promotion of women's empowerment.

The crux of the issue was power and resources. For many within agencies and governments, empowering women meant giving up male power and privilege.[3] Investment in women implied either reallocating existing resources or finding additional sources of revenue. In the absence of women's demonstrated political power as a constituency, the national and international bureaucracies were under no pressure to choose either option.

But building women as a political constituency was difficult. Women are not a homogeneous category, but are differentiated by class, race and nation, and often their choices and opportunities are determined more by these factors than by their gender. While on issues like rights and security women could be united in their stand, other issues such as poverty and entitlement were much more divisive. The movement's failure to take a consistent stand on a core agenda allowed agencies and states to come forward with a partial response. Generally they took measures that did not involve any hard choices, creating underfunded mandates, adding a few projects to their existing portfolios, and supporting research, training and the development of operational tools and techniques. But they shied away from legal and institutional reforms to remove barriers to women's equal participation, and continued to promote macro-policies that exacerbated inequalities between classes and nations. This uneven response by agencies and states explains the mixed results – the heightened advocacy and awareness of gender issues on the one hand, and increased poverty among women on the other. The agencies and governments argued that it was lack of understanding and expertise preventing them from achieving their WID/GAD policy objectives. But they underplayed the political economy of the process of change: how the disparities in power and resources and conflict of interest might obstruct achievement of WID/GAD policy objectives.

The agency WID policies and measures emphasized instrumental objectives, such as integration and mainstreaming, rather than substantive objectives like gender equality and women's empowerment. They gave priority to institutional strategies, in the hope that once institutionalized gender concerns would become legitimate, and they would get routine attention in agency operations and access to regular budget provisions. Some of the efforts bore fruit: WID/gender issues became legitimate concerns in agency discourse and operations. But this emphasis on institutionalization also resulted in WID often losing sight of the women's agenda. Agencies monitored adoption of WID policies and measures, rather than the impact of these measures on the ground in achieving the substantive objectives of gender equality and women's empowerment.

What lessons can be drawn from the experiences of the last two decades? Where do we go from here? One lesson that can be drawn is that in future, policies and measures should more clearly address the women's agenda. Instead of trying to fit gender issues into every sector, the focus should move towards an agenda-setting approach.

FROM AN INTEGRATIONIST TO AN AGENDA-SETTING APPROACH

What will a shift towards an agenda-setting approach involve? It will necessitate changes on many fronts – in decisionmaking structures and processes, in articulation of objectives, in prioritization of strategies, in the positioning of gender issues amidst competing emerging concerns, and in building a mass base of support among both men and women.

Agenda-setting, first of all, implies leadership. Women will have to play a proactive role. This will require a change in existing decision-making structures and processes, which will need to be more inclusive. Women who are affected by development interventions, or their organizations, need to participate in decisionmaking structures, which will need to be made democratic and participatory. Only through a voice in decisionmaking can women aspire to shape the objectives, priorities and strategies of development, and start to transform the development agenda. An agenda-setting approach will naturally imply a focus on agendas, which will involve a clear articulation of a women's core agenda. Since women are not a homogeneous category, such an agenda will have to represent the interests of different classes and groups of women. Policies and interventions would have to address the issues on such a women's agenda. Since the poor and the underprivileged constitute the majority of the world's women, interventions benefiting them will need to be prioritized over measures benefiting more affluent and privileged women.

Within the agencies, an agenda-setting approach will involve greater attention to the substantive objectives of the women's movement: gender equality and women's empowerment. The donors' preoccupation with instrumental objectives – such as integration and mainstreaming, and WID institutionalization – will have to give way to prioritizing operational issues – removing legal and institutional barriers to women's equal participation, and designing and implementing gender-responsive policies and interventions.

An agenda-setting approach will require strategic positioning of gender concerns in a period of change. Within agencies, this will involve linking with and influencing other emerging mandates. Outside the agency, it will require the women's movement to seize the political space being opened up by the emergence of new democracies and the growing strength of civil society. Women are already participating in increasing numbers in citizens' groups and people's movements. This process needs to be strengthened to make women's voices heard, and to mobilize people's support behind the women's agenda. Women's participation in the political process is all the more critical as global economic restructuring threatens to undermine a significant part of the women's agenda, with the emphasis on rolling back the state and free trade and open markets signalling a trend towards a decrease in social safety nets and an increased exploitation of women's cheap labour in productive activities and their unpaid labour in reproduction.

An agenda-setting approach would require giving primacy to women's agency – strengthening women's groups and organizations. These are still weak in many countries, with a narrow base dependent primarily on women's support. In many countries of the South, women's organizations and networks are heavily dependent on external donor funding. Their networking with the international women's movement, particularly with donor organizations, is often stronger than their networking with other organizations in their own countries. In future, women's groups and movements need to enhance their base of popular support, devising strategies to strengthen their financial position and gain male support. In Southern countries, women's organizations need to identify domestic sources of funding.

A new communication strategy is needed to facilitate the expansion of support for the women's movement. Up to now, advocacy of gender issues has been perceived as a 'win/lose' scenario: women's gains have been seen as men's losses. In future, the message should be communicated as a 'win/win' scenario: changing gender roles and relations is good not simply for women – it also benefits men, families and communities, and would create significant inter-generational benefits. Additionally, the communication strategy should target the younger generation much more consciously. Here, advocates of gender equality can learn a lesson from the environmentalists. While the message of environmentalism has caught the imagination of both boys and girls, the message of the women's movement has had much less success with the boys. Indeed, the message of civil rights and equality, in general, has had much less success, despite its affirmation by the constitutions and the legal systems of different nations.

Agenda-setting would also involve the development of concepts and analytical tools in different languages and different development contexts. Concepts and methodologies are powerful tools to control agendas, as they can both include and exclude particular groups. Though many of the conceptual and methodological innovations in WID/GAD have emerged out of grassroots innovations in the South, they have been systematized and packaged primarily in Western academic institutions or in the donor agencies, and in the English language. In future, greater attention needs to be paid to the development of concepts, analytical tools and models in the South. While developing new concepts and models, the women's movement has to be more vigilant in the future against the cooptation of language. Terms such as 'empowerment' are increasingly being used by the conservatives, but their agenda under 'empowerment' is very different from that of the women's movement. The movement has to assess carefully whether, in the name of 'empowerment' and 'responsibility', new policies and interventions are being promoted by the conservatives that will withdraw support and investment and at the same time increase women's burden.

Finally, an agenda-setting approach, in the context of international development assistance, would require building the institutional capacities of aid recipients to set and implement their own agendas. Though the professed objective of donor agencies is to assist the aid recipients in their own efforts to develop themselves, in reality it is in only a very few aid-recipient countries that the agencies have pursued a systematic and sustained effort to build national institutional capacity on gender issues.

SHARED RESPONSIBILITY

Though the development discourse of international agencies has paid routine homage to the notion of global interlinkages and sharing, in reality what has been happening in the global village is not sharing but cost-shifting. In the name of free competition and efficiency, people with power and privilege have been able to shift their costs onto the less privileged, and thus accumulate more. In the last half-century inequalities and disparities have grown rather than lessened. Agenda-setting would involve raising awareness about the need to share responsibilities more equitably in the future – a fair sharing between young and old, women and men, poor and rich, and South and North.

Shared responsibility should be the cornerstone of the new institutions we are trying to create to meet the challenges of the twenty-first century – the new family, community, state and global network. The old family structures are breaking down, primarily because of a male abandonment of responsibility and women's expanded responsibility to earn cash income. The family as an institution cannot be reinvigorated on the basis of the old notion of complementarity of roles: it has to be based on shared roles and responsibilities. An emphasis on 'family values' would imply a reminder to the fathers – whether married or not – about their responsibilities, and the need to shoulder their fair share of the burden.

Communities would have to be rebuilt, again on the principle of shared responsibilities between rich and poor, men and women, public and private sector, and state and community-based organizations. Shared responsibility would imply not simply sharing work and burdens but also a voice in decisionmaking and equitable sharing of resources and revenue. Communities cannot be rebuilt on the notion of abandoning the rural areas and city slums, but only through a fair cost-sharing between rural and urban areas, suburbs and cities, and between rich and poor neighbourhoods.

In recent years, the state and its institutions have also faced increasing scrutiny. Government bureaucracies are criticized for not being efficient, responsive, transparent and accountable; talk of reforming the state and reinventing government is in the air. Again, future reforms of state institutions would have to be grounded in the principle of fair sharing: governments should deliver services to people in proportion to the revenue received from the people; they should be transparent and accountable; and they should share information with citizens and give citizens' groups a voice in influencing decisions. State institutions cannot be energized on the old notion of the state taking on total responsibility on behalf of the people: they would have to be strengthened on the basis of a greater sharing of responsibilities between the government and the non-governmental sector.

Finally, the global institutions and community would have to be restructured on the principle of burden-sharing. This would imply, first of all, a recognition of the unequal burdens on North and South; the net transfer of resources from the South to North through unequal terms of trade. The global institutions and community cannot be restructured on the basis of continued built-in disparities in transactions, but must be created on the principles of justice and fairness. For the women's movement the choice is clear. If the movement truly wants to transform the development agenda, it has to take a consistent stand in favour of fair burden-sharing at all levels – within the family, the community, the nation and the world.

NOTES

1. Johanna Schalkwyk, 'Looking Forward: Some Considerations for WID Strategies', unpublished paper, 1994.

2. Caroline O.N. Moser, *Gender Planning and Development: Theory, Practice and Training*, Routledge, London and New York 1993.

3. Kathleen Staudt, *Women, Foreign Assistance and Advocacy Administration*, Praeger, New York 1985.

APPENDIX

Table A1 NORAD: Gender Distribution of Employees in Oslo Head Office,[1] 1985–92

| | 1985 | | | | 1992 | | | |
| | Men | | Women | | Men | | Women | |
Position	no.	(%)	no.	(%)	no.	(%)	no.	(%)
Director-general, deputy/senior directors	17	(94.4)	1	(5.6)	11	(78.6)	3	(21.4)
Heads of division	14	(70.0)	6	(30.0)	13	(72.2)	5	(27.8)
Senior/special advisors	5	(100.0)	0	(0)	17	(85.0)	3	(15.0)
Senior executive officers	29	(72.5)	11	(27.5)	31	(41.9)	43	(58.1)
Junior executive officers	26	(22.4)	90	(77.6)	9	(18.0)	41	(82.0)
Clerks/ messengers	5	(7.7)	60	(92.3)	7	(17.5)	33	(82.5)
Total	96	(36.4)	168	(63.6)	88	(40.7)	128	(59.3)

Note: [1] Including Ministry of Development Cooperation.
Source: NORAD Statistics Office.

Table A2 NORAD: Gender Distribution of Employees' Resident Representations,[1] 1985–92

Position	1985 Men no.	(%)	Women no.	(%)	1992 Men no.	(%)	Women no.	(%)
Resident representatives	7	(87.5)	1	(12.5)	10	(90.9)	1	(9.1)
Senior project officers	20	(66.7)	10	(33.3)	32	(66.7)	16	(33.3)
Junior project officers	6	(42.9)	8	(57.1)	6	(40.0)	9	(60.0)
Clerks	0	(0)	3	(100.0)	1	(25.0)	3	(75.0)
Total	33	(63.5)	19	(36.5)	49	(62.8)	29	(37.2)

Note: [1] Locally employed personnel not included.
Source: NORAD Statistics Office.

Table A3 UNDP: Distribution of Men and Women in Professional Grade-Levels,[1] 1975–93

Grade	1975 Men	Women	(% women)	1993 Men	Women	(% women)
ADM	–	–	–	1	0	(0)
USG	2	0	(0)	1	0	(0)
ASG	10	0	(0)	6	1	(14)
D-2	86	3	(3)	54	6	(10)
L-7	5	0	(0)	10	0	(0)
D-1	122	9	(6)	117	11	(8)
L-6	6	1	(14)	45	0	(0)
P-5	127	22	(14)	205	56	(21)
L-5	4	1	(20)	115	25	(17)
P-4	61	34	(35)	177	69	(28)
L-4	4	1	(20)	75	21	(21)
P-3	26	30	(53)	112	96	(46)
L-3	1	0	(0)	67	30	(30)
P-2	5	15	(75)	44	53	(54)
L-2	2	2	(50)	26	9	(25)
P-1	0	1	(100)	1	2	(66)
L-1	–	–	–	2	2	(50)
Total	461	119	(20)	1,058	381	(26)

Note: [1] Excluding JPOs.
Source: UNDP HRIC, DOP

Table A4 World Bank: Women's Share in Different Job Categories, 1976–93

Level	1976			1985			1990			1993		
	Total board	Women	% women	Total board	Women	% women	Total board	Women	% women	Total board	Women	% women
31	n.a.	n.a.	(n.a.)	n.a.	n.a.	(n.a.)	1	0	(0.0)	2	0	(0.0)
30	n.a.	n.a.	(n.a.)	n.a.	n.a.	(n.a.)	7	0	(0.0)	4	0	(0.0)
29	18	0	(0)	27	1	(3.7)	16	0	(0.0)	17	1	(5.9)
28	64	1	(0.5)	53	0	(0.0)	83	3	(3.6)	70	7	(10.0)
27	78	0	(0)	79	3	(3.8)	52	2	(3.8)	52	3	(5.8)
26	209	2	(0.9)	336	10	(3.0)	366	26	(7.1)	355	40	(11.3)
25	n.a.	n.a.	(n.a.)	n.a.	n.a.	(n.a.)	412	25	(6.1)	414	44	(10.6)
24	436	10	(4.7)	1136	78	(6.9)	1191	168	(14.1)	1211	210	(15.3)
23	n.a.	n.a.	(n.a.)	1067	184	(17.2)	814	195	(24.0)	781	208	(26.6)
22	n.a.	n.a.	(n.a.)	312	101	(32.4)	331	110	(33.2)	325	147	(44.8)
21	n.a.	n.a.	(n.a.)	74	38	(51.4)	177	96	(54.2)	191	94	(49.2)
20	n.a.	n.a.	(n.a.)	62	35	(56.5)	201	131	(65.2)	221	145	(65.6)
19	n.a.	n.a.	(n.a.)	277	100	(65.0)	269	178	(66.2)	187	134	(71.7)
18	n.a.	n.a.	(n.a.)	401	267	(66.6)	151	106	(68.5)	100	69	(69.8)
YP	n.a.	n.a.	(n.a.)	27	13	(48.1)	34	10	(29.4)	30	19	(63.3)
UHL	n.a.	n.a.	(n.a.)	62	22	(35.5)	31	6	(19.4)	38	6	(15.8)
Total HL				3913	932	(23.8)	4136	1055	(25.5)	4000	1127	(28.7)

Note: All dates refer to the relevant fiscal years.

Source: 1976 data: 'Bank/IFC Appointment-Based HL Staff Statistics', Annual Meeting brief, PAAVP, 31 August 1988; 1985, 1990 data: 'Human Resources Data Annual Review FY91'; 1993 data: Personnel Department, World Bank, 1993.

BIBLIOGRAPHY

Acharya, Meena and Bennett, Lynn, *Women and the Subsistence Sector: Economic Participation and the Household Decision Making*, World Bank 1982.

Afshar, Haleh, ed., *Women, Work and Ideology in the Third World*, Tavistock, London 1985.

———— *Women, State and Ideology: Studies from Africa and Asia*, State University of New York Press, Albany 1987.

Beneria, Lourdes, ed., *Women and Development: The Sexual Division of Labour in Rural Societies*, Praeger, New York, and ILO, Geneva, 1982.

Boserup, Ester, *Women's Role in Economic Development*, St Martin's Press, New York 1970.

Boserup, Ester and Liljencrantz, Christina, *Integration of Women in Development – Why, When, How*, UNDP, 1975.

Boulding, Elise, *Women in the Twentieth-Century World*, John Wiley & Sons, New York 1977.

Buvinic, Mayra, 'Project for Women in the Third World: Explaining their Misbehaviour', *World Development*, vol. 14, no. 5, 1986.

Buvinic, Mayra and Youssef, H. Nadia, with Barbara von Elm, 'Women-Headed Households: The Ignored Factor in Development Planning', USAID, Washington DC, and ICRW Report, 1978.

Buvinic, Mayra, et al., *Women and Poverty in the Third World*, Johns Hopkins University Press, Baltimore 1983.

Canadian International Development Agency (CIDA), *Women in Development Policy Framework*, mimeo, n.d.

———— *A Handbook for Social/Gender Analysis*, n.d.

———— Annual Report, 1987–88, 1988–89, 1989–90.

———— *Annual Report of the WID Steering Committee to the Presidents' Committee*, 1988, 1989, 1990, 1991.

———— *CIDA Action Plan for Equal Opportunities for Women*, 1975.

———— *Equal Opportunities for Women: Five-Year Action Plan*, 1983.

———— *Guidelines for Integrating WID into Project Design and Evaluation*, 1986.

———— *Women in Development: CIDA Action Plan*, 1986.

———— *Employment Equity Progress Report*, 1987–88.

———— *Organization and Human Resources Planning: Annual Report 1988–89*.

———— *Asia Program: Women in Development Strategy*, 1989.

———— *Women: A Vital Force in Development*, 1989.

———— *Women in Development and the Project Cycle*, September 1989.

———— *Women in Development: A Sectoral Perspective*, 1989.

———— *Asia WID Co-ordinators' Regional Meeting*, Singapore, 1990.

——— *Status Report on the Integration of Women in Technical Co-operation, Scholarship and Training Activities*, January 1990.

——— *Women in Development Program: Evaluation Assessment Report*, 21 December 1990.

——— *CIDA: Women in Development Framework*, Draft, October 1991.

——— *Strategic Management Review*, 1991.

——— *Women in Development and Gender Equity*, Administrative Notice A 1096-2, 1991.

——— *Women in Development Co-ordinators' Orientation and Training: Final Report*, July 1991.

——— *Agency Action Plan for the Employment Equity Program 1991–93* (Draft).

——— *Gender as a Cross Cutting Theme in Development Assistance – An Evaluation of CIDA's WID Policy and Activities, 1984–1992*, July 1993.

Carloni, A., 'Integrating Women in Agriculture Projects: Case Studies of Ten FAO-assisted Field Projects', FAO, Rome 1983.

Commonwealth Secretariat, *Engendering Adjustment in the 1990s*, Report of the Commonwealth Expert Group on Women and Structural Adjustment, 1990.

Dixon, Ruth, *Women's Work in Third World Agriculture*, ILO, Geneva 1985.

Dwyer, Daisy, and Bruce, Judith, eds., *A Home Divided: Women and Income in the Third World*, Stanford University Press, Stanford 1988.

Elson, Diane, 'Gender Issues in Development Strategies', paper presented at a seminar on the Integration of Women in Development, Vienna, 9–11 December 1991.

FAO, *Second Progress Report on WCAARRD Programme of Action Including the Role of Women in Rural Development*, Rome 1987.

Gordon, S., ed., 'Ladies in Limbo: the Fate of Women's Bureaux', Six Case Studies from the Caribbean, Commonwealth Secretariat, Human Resources Development Group Women and Development Programme, London 1985.

Government of Bangladesh, *The Fourth Five-Year Plan, 1990–95*.

Halsas, Beatrice, 'Policies and Strategies on Women in Norway', 1989.

Hayter, Teresa, *Aid as Imperialism*, Penguin, Harmondsworth 1971.

Herz, Barbara and Measham, R. Anthony, *The Safe Motherhood Initiative*, The World Bank, 1987.

Herz, Barbara, et al., *Letting Girls Learn*, The World Bank, 1991.

Heyzer, Noeleen, ed., *Women Farmers in Rural Change in Asia*, APDC, Kuala Lumpur 1987.

Hooper, Emma, *Status Report of Selected World Bank Projects Benefiting Women*, The World Bank, November 1988.

Hossain, Mahbub and Afsar, Rita, *Credit for Women's Involvement in Economic Activities in Rural Bangladesh*, BIDS, Dhaka, December 1988.

Jahan, Rounaq and Papanek, Hanna, eds., *Women and Development: Perspectives from South and South East Asia*, BILIA, Dhaka 1979.

——— 'Women and Development in Bangladesh: Challenges and Opportunities', The Ford Foundation, Dhaka 1989.

——— 'Mainstreaming Women in Development in Different Settings', paper presented at a seminar on Mainstreaming Women in Development, Paris, 18–19 May 1992.

Jahan, Roushan, 'Women's Movement in Bangladesh: Concerns and Challenges', *Alternatives*, vol. II, DAWN, 1991.

Jensen, G. Eirik, 'Interest Groups and Development Assistance: The Case of Bangladesh', in *SQKJELYSPAU HJELPA*, 1992.

Jiggins, Janet, 'Consultancy Report on Bangladesh', mimeo, World Bank, 1987.

Joekes, Susan P., *Women in the World Economy: An INSTRAW Study*, Oxford University Press, New York and Oxford 1987.

—— 'Gender and Macro-Economic Policy', mimeo, Institute of Development Studies, University of Sussex, 1988.

Joekes, Susan; Lycette, Margaret; Macgowan, Lisa and Searle, Karan, 'Women and Structural Adjustment', mimeo, ICRW, 1988.

Jorstad, Mette, *Is Pipeline the Problem in Planning Projects Against Poverty: The WID Issue and Target Group Orientation in Mainly Infrastructure Projects*, MDC, Oslo, November 1987.

Kardam, Nuket, *Bringing Women In: Women's Issues in International Development Programmes*, Reinner Publishers, Boulder and London 1991.

King, Elizabeth M., *Educating Girls and Women: Investing in Development*, The World Bank, 1990.

Kossoudji, Sherrie and Mueller, Eva, *The Economic and Demographic Status of Female-Headed Households in Rural Botswana*, Population Studies Center, University of Michigan, Ann Arbor 1981.

Lewis, C. Barbara, ed., *Invisible Farmers: Women and the Crisis in Agriculture*, USAID, Washington DC 1981.

Lexow, Janne, *WID Issues in Norwegian Development Assistance*, MDC, Oslo, January 1987.

—— *WID Issues in Nordic Development Assistance*, MDC, Oslo, March 1988.

Lexow, Janne and McNeill, Desmond, *The Women's Grant*, Evaluation Report 2.89, MDC, Oslo, February 1989.

Lexow, Janne and Skjonsberg, Else, *Good Aid for Women? A Review of Women's Issues in Three Selected Norwegian Bilateral Development Projects*, MDC, Oslo, February 1989.

Lycklama, Geartje, 'The Fallacy of Integration: The UN Strategy of Integrating Women into Development Revisited', paper presented to the development policy seminar for UNDP staff, The Hague, November 1987.

—— *Towards Women's Strategies in the 1990s: Challenging Government and the State*, Macmillan, London 1991.

Lwanga-Okwenge, Elizabeth, Statement before the Economic and Social Council, mimeo, 1992.

McAllister, Elizabeth, *Managing the Process of Change: Women in Development*, CIDA, 1989.

The Royal Norwegian Ministry of Development Co-operation (MDC), *Norway's Strategy for Assistance to Women in Development*, 1985.

—— *Women in Norwegian Bilateral Development Co-operation*, Oslo, April 1988.

Mies, Maria, *Patriarchy and Accumulation on a World Scale. Women in the International Division of Labour*, Zed Books, London 1986.

Mitter, Swasti, *Common Fate, Common Bond: Women in the Global Economy*, Pluto, London 1986.

Molner, Angusta and Schreiber, Gotz, *Women and Forestry: Operational Issues,* The World Bank, 1989.

Molyneux, Maxine, 'Women's Emancipation Under Socialism: A Model for the Third World', *World Development,* vol. 9, no. 10, 1981.

Moser, Caroline O.N., *Gender Planning and Development: Theory, Practice and Training,* Routledge, London and New York 1993.

Nash, June and Fernandez-Kelly, Maria Patricia, eds., *Women, Men and the International Division of Labour,* State University of New York Press, Albany 1983.

Norwegian Agency for Development Cooperation (NORAD), *Bi and Multilateral Co-operation,* n.d.

——— *The Logical Framework Approach (LFA): Handbook for Objective-Oriented Project Planning,* Oslo, n.d.

——— *Handlingsplan for Kvinnerett et Bistand,* November 1984.

——— *Department et For Utviklingshjelp's Arbeid Med Kvinnerett et Bistand,* 1986–88.

——— *Action Plan for Women in Development: Bangladesh,* Dhaka, 1987.

——— *NORAD's Handlingsplan: Status for Gjennomforing,* June 1987.

——— *Action Plan for Women in Development, Tanzania,* Dar-es Salaam, 1989.

——— *Environmental Impact Assessment (EIA) of Development Aid Projects,* Oslo, December 1989.

——— *Action Plan for WID, Bangladesh,* First Revision, Draft, 1990.

——— *NORAD and Norwegian Bilateral Development Co-operation,* Oslo, 1990.

——— *Strategies for Development Co-operation: NORAD in the Nineties,* Oslo, September 1990.

——— 'Agreed Minutes Country Programme Consultations between Tanzania and Norway', mimeo, 4–8 April 1991.

Organization for Economic Cooperation and Development (OECD), Development Assistance Committee (DAC), *From Nairobi to the Year 2000 – Actions Proposed for DAC Member Countries to Fulfil their Commitment to the Nairobi Forward Looking Strategies,* May 1981.

——— *Aid Review, 1988–1989: Memorandum of Norway,* Paris, July 1989.

——— *Methodology for Statistical Reporting of Women Oriented Aid Activities,* 1989.

——— *Memorandum of Canada Aid Review 1988/89.*

——— Expert Group on Women in Development, *Third Monitoring Report on the Implementation of the DAC Revised Guiding Principles on WID, 1989,* Paris, May 1990.

——— *Aid Review, 1989–1990: Memorandum of Norway,* Paris, April 1990.

——— *Aid Review, 1990–1991: Memorandum of Norway,* Paris, August 1990.

——— *Memorandum of Canada Aid Review 1989/90.*

Overholt, Catherine, et al., eds., *Gender Roles in Development Projects,* Kumarian Press, West Hartford 1985.

Pietila, Hilkka and Eide, Ingrid, *United Nations and the Advancement of Women: The Role of the Nordic Countries in the Advancement of Women Within the United Nations System,* The Nordic UN Project Report no. 16, 1990.

Lund, Ragnhild, *Evaluation of NORAD Projects and Effects on Women,* NORAD, 1978.

Rao, Aruna, et al., eds., *Gender Training and Development Planning: Learning from Experience,* Population Council and Christian Michelsten Institute, 1992.

Rogers, Barbara, *The Domestication of Women: Discrimination in Developing Societies*, St Martin's Press, New York 1979.

Schultz, T. Paul, *Women and Development: Objectives, Policy Framework and Policy Interventions*, April 1989.

———— *Women's Changing Participation in the Labor Force*, The World Bank Working Paper, 1989.

Sen, Gita and Grown, Caren, *Development, Crises and Alternative Visions: Third World Women's Perspectives*, Monthly Review Press, New York 1987.

Standing, Guy, 'Global Feminization through Flexible Labour', *World Development*, July 1989, pp. 1077–96.

Staudt, Kathleen, *Women, Foreign Assistance and Advocacy Administration*, Praeger, New York 1985.

Staudt, Kathleen, ed., *Women, International Development and Politics: The Bureaucractic Mire*, Temple University Press, Philadelphia 1990.

Tendler, Judith, *Inside Foreign Aid*, Johns Hopkins University Press, Baltimore 1975.

———— 'What Ever Happened to Poverty Alleviation?', *World Development*, July 1989, pp. 1033–44.

Tinker, Irene, ed., *Women in Washington: Advocates for Public Policy*, Pergamon Press, New York, Sage, London 1983.

———— *Persistent Inequalities*, Oxford University Press, New York 1990,

Tinker, Irene and Bramsen, Michelle B., eds., *Women and World Development*, ODC, Washington DC 1976.

Tinker, Irene and Jaquette, Jane, 'UN Decade for Women: Its Impact and Legacy', *World Development*, 1987, vol. 15, no. 3, pp. 419–27.

UNICEF, *An Analysis of the Situation of Children in Bangladesh*, Dhaka 1987.

United Nations (UN) International Women's Year Secretariat, Meeting in Mexico: *World Conference of the International Women's Year 1975*, New York: Center for Economic and Social Information, 1975.

———— *World Plan of Action for the Implementation of the Objectives of the International Women's Year*, New York, 1975.

———— *Programme of Action for the Second Half of the United Nations Decade for Women: Equality, Development and Peace*. A/Conf. 94/34, New York, 13 August 1980.

———— *The Nairobi Forward-Looking Strategies for the Advancement of Women*, United Nations Department of Public Information, Division for Economic and Social Information, April 1986.

———— *World Survey on the Role of Women in Development*, New York 1989.

United Nations Development Programme (UNDP), *Guidelines on the Integration of Women in Development*, G3100-1, 25 February 1977.

UNDP, *Integration of Women in Development – Implementation of Governing Council Decision 80/22/II*, UNDP/PROG/79; UNDP/PROG/FIELD/120, 12 February 1981.

———— *Women's Participation in Development: An Inter-Organizational Assessment*, Evaluation Study 13, New York, June 1985.

———— *Programme Implementation – Women in Development Strategy*, DP/1986/14, 26 February 1986.

―――― Bureau for Programme and Policy Evaluation, *Draft UNDP Programme Advisory Note: Women in Development*, mimeo, May 1986.

―――― *Programme Implementation – The Implementation of Decision Adopted by the Governing Council at Previous Sessions: Women in Development*, DP/1987/15, 20 April 1987.

―――― 'Women in UNDP-Supported Projects: A Review of How UNDP Project Evaluations Deal with Gender Issues', New York, May 1987.

―――― 'Women in Development Policy and Procedures', mimeo, 17 November 1987.

―――― *Women in Development – Project Achievement Reports from the UNDP*, New York, June 1988.

―――― Governing Council, *Programme Implementation – Implementation of Decision Adopted by the Governing Council at Previous Sessions: Women in Development*, DP/1989/24, 15 March 1989.

―――― *Women in Development: Report of the Administrator*, 30 April 1990.

USAID and DDA, *Assessment of Policies and Organizational Measures in Women in Development Adopted by DAC Member Countries*, mimeo, 1994.

Wellesley Editorial Committee, ed., *Women and National Development: The Complexities of Change*, University of Chicago Press, Chicago 1977.

Women for Women, *Women and National Planning in Bangladesh*, Dhaka 1990.

World Bank, *Bangladesh: Strategies for Enhancing the Role of Women in Economic Development*, 1980.

―――― *Annual Report*, 1989

―――― *Kenya: The Role of Women in Economic Development*, 1989.

―――― *Women in Development Issues for Economic and Sector Analysis*, 1989.

―――― *Women in Pakistan: An Economic and Social Strategy*, 1989.

―――― *Annual Report*, 1990

―――― *Women in Development: A Progress Report on the World Bank Initiative*, 1990.

―――― *Annual Report*, 1991

―――― *Excellence through Equality: An Increased Role for Women in the World Bank: A Report of the Advisory Group on Higher Level Women's Issues*, April 1992.

World Bank Staff Association, *Report on Status of Higher Level Women in the World Bank Group*, November 1989.

INDEX

DATE DUE

DEMCO